W.H. Hutt:
An Economist for the Long Run

A Festschrift
edited by
Morgan O. Reynolds

Gateway Editions

Chicago   Washington, DC

Regnery Books is a Division of Regnery
Gateway, Inc. All inquiries concerning this
book should be directed to Regnery Books, 950
North Shore Drive, Lake Bluff, IL 60044.

Published for and in association with
The Heritage Foundation, Washington DC.

Library of Congress Cataloging-in-Publication Data

W.H. Hutt: an economist for the long run.

  "Published for and in association with the
Heritage Foundation, Washington D.C."—T.p.
verso.
  1. Hutt, W. H. (William Harold), 1899–
2. Economists—Great Britain—
Biography. 3. Laissezfaire. 4. Social
justice. 5. Economic policy.
I. Reynolds, Morgan, O., 1942-   . II. Hutt,
W. H. (William Harold), 1899-   .
III. Heritage Foundation (Washington, D.C.)
HB103.H93W18 1986   330′.092′4 [B] 86-42794
ISBN: 0-89526-797-7

TABLE OF CONTENTS

FOREWORD

For almost 60 years, W. H. Hutt has labored in undeserved obscurity. Although he has done seminal work in a dozen or more areas of economics, his name rarely appears in textbooks or among those receiving the awards and accolades of the economics profession. This is a tragedy, because Bill Hutt is one of the few original thinkers in the field of economics in this century. He originated the concept of "consumer sovereignty," developed the first comprehensive theory of idle resources, and the first coherent theory of collective bargaining.

In addition to his original contributions to economic theory, Hutt also contributed to economic understanding by elaborating on the great truths of the classical economics, as in his book on Say's Law. He also added to our understanding by helping refute the fallacies of Keynesian economics. And he has also engaged in regular debate on issues of policy. His book on South African apartheid stands as a monument to clear thinking in an area in which little appears on any side.

Despite his lack of recognition and shabby treatment by the academic establishment, Bill Hutt has remained throughout a cheerful and engaging teacher and lecturer, a prolific writer, and a staunch defender of freedom. He was a founding member of the Mont Pelerin Society and a great influence not only on my own thinking, but on that of a generation of free market thinkers. Fortunately, most of us did not have to wait as long as Bill Hutt to see the renaissance in classical, free market thinking which is now sweeping the world. Those of us who are working daily to undo the shackles of government, whether in Washington for the Reagan Administration, in London for the Thatcher Government, or in such unlikely places as Paris or even Beijing, owe an enormous debt to people like W. H. Hutt—a debt which can never be adequately repaid.

This small volume may help repay, in a small way, our generation's debt to Bill Hutt.

Edwin J. Feulner, Jr.
President
The Heritage Foundation

AN INTRODUCTION TO W.H. HUTT: AN ECONOMIST FOR THE LONG RUN

Can a great—and greatly neglected—economist win vindication in his lifetime? If he lives to a ripe old age and his adversaries keep showing how wrong they are, the chances seem good, judged by a sample of one. To wit, William Harold Hutt turned 87 in August, 1986, his adversaries continue to oblige with numerous errors and the stirrings of vindication are unmistakable.

The general signs of intellectual renewal are all around us and amid the wreckage of Keynesian economics, a Hutt revival is underway. Bill was among the precious few that kept economic truth alive and growing in the dismal period since Lord Keynes sought to do good to the world with his pen. While Keynes hungered for influence and achieved it—telling articulate opinion what it wanted to hear—Hutt did no such thing. Bill Hutt pursued the truth, no matter where it led. And now we see the signs that the truth will out in the end, at least in a relatively open society, even for the many who do not pursue it. Hutt's truths pursue them. Hutt's many books are now being hailed as landmarks and it is virtually impossible to find a reputable Keynesian under the age of 45 in the United States, so far as I can tell.

Lest I be too effusive, I must admit that we have a great distance to go yet. Hutt's teachings are hardly the main course at MIT, Harvard and Yale or in the major political parties. But maybe, just maybe, this volume will find its way into the right hands—more importantly, minds—and play a small but vital role in shifting the grounds of debate in the academy and ultimately in policy.

Hutt's key ideas—that fiscal and monetary policy cannot overcome pricing defects, that restraints on competition impoverish the poor and the disadvantaged, that only pricing can coordinate and restore employment and output, that government concessions to sectionalist interest groups harm the social interest, that every increase in output adds to the source of demands for noncompeting outputs, that free markets maximize employment and output and diminish inequality—no longer wander as intellectual outcasts. They are no longer beyond consideration in civilized quarters. In Texanese, you just can't beat a little man who keeps on a comin', especially if he's right.

Perhaps I should answer a question that relatively few (translation: no one) have asked me: how did this festschrift to honor Bill Hutt and his work come about? John O'Sullivan, then editor of *Policy Review,* called me in the summer of 1982 and said that the Heritage Foundation was arranging such a volume. Would I be willing to contribute a piece on race relations and the colour bar? My answer was, of course, what a marvelous idea, I'd be delighted. John told me that he had received commitments from Arthur Shenfield and Ralph Horwitz as well. I was to have my paper prepared by mid-October and in view of Bill Hutt's advanced years and frail health, the volume would be readied as soon as possible.

So much for urgency. I submitted my paper by November 1982, almost on time, and patted myself on the back for a job well done. John O'Sullivan, however, left Heritage shortly thereafter to resume journalism on the other side of the pond and the project seemed to grind to a halt. Quite independently, meanwhile, the *Manhattan Report* devoted an issue to Hutt in 1983, Tom Hazlett did an article for *The Wall Street Journal* on Hutt, and I did an interview with Hutt for the *Journal of Labor Research* (the latter two articles are included here). My thought was that it would be a shame not to publish the present volume,

so I pursued it. Though not the original in-
spiration but rather a carpet-bagging editor on this project, I am immensely
pleased and satisfied with the result. Everyone connected with this project deserves kudos. The authors and publisher,
certainly, but I would like to single out two
less visible participants for special thanks:
Ed Feulner for his intellectual and financial support, and his assistant—Bridgett
Wagner—for her cheerful perseverance.
Thanks.

One final note. A colleague of mine, John
Lott, Jr., proofed the manuscript and suggested an article on Hutt's *Theory of Idle
Resources.* Why? Because around UCLA
Armen Alchian apparently used to say
that Hutt's *Idle Resources* was one of the
three most important books on economics.
Hutt anticipated Stigler's theory of information and search by decades, exposed the
fallacies in Keynes's theory of unemployment, and so on. In the interests of publishing something sooner rather than later,
however, I decided to proceed with the volume you see now rather than delay it any
longer. In my opinion, the moral is that the
timeless quality of Hutt's work has not
been exhausted, only touched, by this festschrift.

Morgan Reynolds
College Station, Texas
May, 1986

RAZING KEYNES:
AN ECONOMIST FOR THE
LONG RUN

by
Thomas Hazlett

W.H. Hutt is 87 years old and may be the most important economist of this century. That this is too little known is in great part a result of his choice. He didn't stay in England.

Instead, in 1928 the young Ph.D. from the London School of Economics set sail for South Africa, where the University of Capetown, and the eminent economist Sir Arnold Plant, beckoned. Safely tucked away down under, Mr. Hutt was to enjoy an impressive scholarly career, knocking out what were to become classics among a select cadre of followers: "The Theory of Collective Bargaining" (1930), "Economists and the Public" (1936), "A Plan for Reconstruction" (1943) and "The Economics of the Colour Bar" (1964). But South Africa is a very long way from any place the truly civilized tread. Mr. Hutt's work stayed strictly non-required reading for the many.

That was a boon to the career of Lord

Keynes. For Mr. Hutt's "Theory of Idle Resources" is an articulate, steady and sweeping intellectual junket over just the same waters traversed by the General Theory. It represents a "clearly superior theory," in the words of economist James Buchanan.

But Keynes's theory won the day. "For one thing," notes Mr. Buchanan, "Hutt was writing from South Africa. More importantly, Keynes gave economists and politicians an argument they wanted to hear . . . Hutt was much more analytically sound, but the classical medicine was harder to accept."

Mr. Hutt carefully constructs a truly general theory of resource idleness, of which the unemployment of labor is a special case. Unlike Keynes's vogue, Mr. Hutt's classically oriented theory is now enjoying a better following than at any time since it was written. In a day when $200 billion deficits coexist with 10% unemployment, "aggregate demand" theories of unemployment leave Keynes's own intellectual offspring cold.

Mr. Hutt's thesis has always been that involuntary unemployment, far from being a question of insufficient demand, results from "defects in the pricing system." Mr. Hutt built on Say's Law (which, he maintains, Keynes twisted in order to destroy: Say didn't mean that an increase in the supply of, say, plums creates additional demand for plums, but rather, demand for whatever the supplier wishes to acquire in exchange for the plums). Mr. Hutt demonstrated that "aggregate demand" and "aggregate supply" are actually identical values looked at from different directions, even in a modern, money-based economy. Hence, "problems arise, not because demand is too low, but because the prices of some goods and the services of much labor, are priced too high. Because these prices are too high, then people do not have sufficient income to purchase the full flow of goods and services."

Keynes's contribution to the employment mystery was to devise a model of the world in which flexible wages (and prices) would *not* lead to full employment. In reducing their wage demands, workers would only shrink aggregate demand, thus frustrating their employment prospects still further. "Thus," wrote Mr. Hutt, "Leon Keyserling (a member of the Council of Economic Advisers) actually urged labour unions in the United States in 1949, to press for increased wage-rates in order to boost effective demand and prevent unemployment."

But, in another of his important books ("Keynesianism: Retrospect and Prospect," 1963) Mr. Hutt dissected the fallacy: "The Keynesians failed to see that the cutting of prices in any field is simply the creation of an additional demand for non-competing goods—because power to purchase is released for other purposes... because [they] have failed to perceive the meaning of coordination thru price adjustment...they think of price-cutting as income cutting."

The policy solution is not to attempt to inject inflationary demand into the economy to prop up an otherwise unsustainable system of relative prices (which will only require more and more inflation over time), but to reduce the cost of necessary market adjustments by stabilizing the value of the monetary unit and refusing to protect any form of labor cartel or monopolistic restriction.

In fact, it was Mr. Hutt's tome on collective bargaining that poignantly described general antilabor consequences of unions, showing that whatever gains might be taken by labor cartels for their members would inevitably (a) reduce aggregate supply, (b) increase the supply of workers in nonunionized employments and, hence, (c) lower real wages for all other workers. Of necessity, this loss to nonunion workers would exceed the gains to the protected workers. As Arthur Seldon, who read Mr. Hutt's book while a doctoral student at the London School in the mid-1930's, remembers it, the volume "effectively destroyed the Fabian argument on labor's disadvantage in the bargaining process."

Yet, enlightened citadels of north Atlantic

scholarship had little trouble in dealing with Mr. Hutt's piercing challenges to mainstream thought: *Silencia.* When pressed, of course, academics could produce a devastating verdict on the poor Prof. Hutt in an instant; he was critically vulnerable to the charge of unrepentant Toryism. If Mr. Hutt knew of the Anglo-American foreign policy toward him, however, he must have found it curious. For in his South African environs, the political ax was falling from just the other side: So doggedly annoying were his economic and classical liberal attacks on apartheid in scholarly forums and the popular press that the white supremacist government was at one point moved to deprive Mr. Hutt of his travel visa.

"The Economics of the Colour Bar" provides an analytical accounting of the economics and sociology of apartheid. This fascinating study, in the words of economist Mancur Olsen, "points out what I had never imagined; that in the early days of the Dutch settlement, there was a surprising amount of of interaction between the Dutch and the Africans and nothing like the present system of apartheid. Hutt shows that, starting in the early twentieth century, particularly after strikes in the gold and diamond mines, there emerged a pattern of cartelization of white laborers in unions whose object was the creation and preservation of a monopoly position by prohibiting and excluding employers from training blacks to be competitors with them."

The Colour Bar Acts, reserving jobs for whites on a quota basis, argues Mr. Hutt, were not as pernicious in their effect as legislation passed simultaneously: "rate of the job," what we would call "equal pay for equal work." This mandate, adopted in the 1920s made lower skilled blacks simply non-employable throughout the skilled portion of the South African economy.

But if Mr. Hutt has been an eyewitness to the cynical use of "progressive, pro–labor" legislation, he may indeed have the last laugh. Now professor emeritus at the University of Dallas, Mr. Hutt may manage an occasional grin to read of contemporary economists and labor leaders alike pushing for greater wage flexibility to maintain employment—or even a full-blown smirk upon learning of yet another Keynesian theorist demanding tax boosts to close the deficit and put Americans back to work. Perhaps being analytically correct is small artillery in the face of an academic theory equipped with power-seeking missiles. If so, at least Mr. Hutt has lived right through and beyond the mistakes of one generation—and his economic masterpieces will live through those of many more.

Reprinted with permission of *The Wall Street Journal*

AN INTERVIEW WITH
W.H. HUTT

On May 17, 1984 Morgan O. Reynolds, a Texas A&M University economist, interviewed W.H. Hutt at his home in Irving, Texas, at the request of James Bennett, editor of the *Journal of Labor Research (JLR)*. An edited transcript follows:

JLR: Professor Hutt, could you begin by telling us about your origins, a little about your mother and father, when and where you were born?

Hutt: I was born in the last century, the 3rd of August, 1899. I was born of a working class family in London, England. My father was a compositor. He was a well educated man; he left school at the age of 12, but when he left school he could do problems in arithmetic which very few children in the United States could do today, even at the age of 16. He could calculate square roots and cube roots, and he was very well read; for instance, he bought the complete works of Charles Dickens, which he purchased out of his meager earnings as a compositor.

JLR: Was he a union member?

Hutt: He was a union member, reluctantly, but he had to be in order to be employed by his company, which was the famous firm of W.H. Smith & Son. We were very well brought up, but we lived frugally, we lived within our income. That doesn't mean there were hardships, not at all. Our alternatives were not as broad as we would have liked them to be, of course. Every year we went on a holiday somewhere, very often to our favorite place, Littlehampton, on the South Coast of Britain. We could afford a fortnight, a two week holiday. At home, we ate cheap foods, good foods. There was no hardship. We certainly never thought in terms of anything being a hardship. We believed in cutting our coat according to our cloth. My father was a very good influence and so was my mother, in that respect. My father, although a heavy smoker, cut out liquor. He refused to go to the parties which his fellow workers organized in the local pubs.

JLR: Why?

Hutt: He thought their general attitude of hostility towards the firms that employed them was absurd. But he thought of all politicians as scoundrels, although on one occasion he actually was inveigled into serving on a local conservative committee in a vain attempt to get Conway Wertheimer elected as a conservative candidate. Immediately after the election, my father resigned from the committee, and took no further part in politics.

JLR: Then you graduated from high school?

Hutt: I had a splendid education in the cheapest, free schools, the London County Council Board Schools, as they were called. I think in the highest terms of the efficiency and dedication of the teachers. There was no teachers' union in those days.

JLR: Did you have brothers and sisters?

Hutt: I had two brothers, both of whom are dead. One died at the age of about eight of heart trouble and the other died of leukemia about ten years ago. My sister, who is 18 months older than me, is still living in South Africa.

JLR: What did your brother who lived to adulthood do for a living?

Hutt: He was in business as a clerk; he was not academic at all.

JLR: That brings us to 1916.

Hutt: Yes, during World War I, I had to join up and I chose the Royal Flying Corps. I was admitted as a Cadet and trained as a pilot, but I missed my RFC wings by a few months. I left with RAF wings in November of 1918. As far as I was concerned, the sooner I got back into civilian life the better, because I perceived that if I was to do anything in life, I would have to start young. I thought at first of getting into some business or other. But then I was made aware of the new degree which had just been founded in the University of London, called the B.Com. degree. I registered for that and was among the first students registered.

JLR: Was this a four year program and did you take economics courses?

Hutt: Yes, that's what the B.Com. degree consisted of in those days. The framers of the degree had no concept at all of the teaching of administration or business administration. It was largely an academic degree, apart from accounting and mercantile law, which were very well taught.

JLR: Were there any Professors whose names we might recognize?

Hutt: In respect of commerce, as such, no. The professor was a chap called Sargent and I think his courses were worthless. He was a classical scholar. I think he was chosen by Beveridge, who was the Director of the School of Economics. Beveridge accepted the prejudices of the day and did not believe that businessmen were capable of teaching other people to be businessmen. He thought that a classical scholar, one expert in Greek and Latin, could.

JLR: Then you went into publishing?

Hutt: After graduation, I was sent by the appointments committee of the University of London to interview with Sir Ernest Benn of Benn Brothers, Ltd., and of Ernest Benn, Ltd. He asked me in the interview what my father did. I told him my father was a compositor, an ordinary compositor. Surely he is the head of his department, Benn asked? I said no, W.H. Smith & Son would never have appointed a man who believed that the unions were tyrannical, which is what my father believed. My father had to accept that he must join the union or the firm would certainly dismiss him; he had to support a union movement that he did not believe in.

JLR: Even though there were no formal, legal obligations to join, only social pressure?

Hutt: Yes. He thought that the managers of W.H. Smith & Son were weak-kneed.

JLR: Like a lot of them today in America?

Hutt: Yes.

JLR: What happened in the interview?

Hutt: Benn rang the overseer at W.H. Smith & Son and asked about Hutt. The answer was that he was a very gentlemanly person, quiet, but very fierce when it came to political issues. In these things he was a nonconformist and he made the union realize that he belonged to it by force. That was just what Benn wanted to hear. I got the job just like that, I told the truth, and from my short association with Benn I gained a great deal.

JLR: What did you do at Benn?

Hutt: I was employed as a personal assistant to Sir Ernest Benn. The company published technical journals, for example, *The Cabinet Maker, The Hardware Trades* journal, *The Gas World,* and so forth. The book publishing side—Ernest Benn Ltd.— was under Victor Gollancz, from the University of Oxford and typically a leftist, of course, condemning the capitalist system, just the opposite of Benn. That association broke up, and I think I helped. We were sent the typed script of a book on family endowment by Eleanor Rathbone. The book was very critical of the family endowment, a name for state welfare, and I thought it was a very good book. It was an attack on the notion of the welfare state. Gollancz said that it was the sort of contribution that he could not handle. Benn turned to me and said, could you get it published? I said yes, P.S. King will accept it. And they did accept it.

JLR: Did they publish a lot of so-called conservative or anti-collectivist books?

Hutt: No, they didn't. They chose their books solely in accordance with profit-making.

JLR: Didn't you publish an article about then?

Hutt: I wrote my first academic article in 1925 and published it in Economica in 1926. It was entitled "The Factory System of the Early Nineteenth Century." It is reprinted in Hayek's *Capitalism and the Historians*. To this day I still get royalties for something that I wrote in 1925, about $30 or $40 a year. That's what is unique about it. I showed the article to Benn and he made hundreds of copies of it and distributed it to his friends. Then he established me as the manager of the Individualist Book Club Ltd., which was in the great book selling road of London, Charing Cross Road. After about 18 months there I got an invitation from the University of Cape Town.

JLR: How did that come about?

Hutt: I happened to see an announcement that they were looking for a Senior Lecturer, and the head of the department in Cape Town was a great friend of mine named Arnold Plant, who later became Sir Arnold Plant. I applied for the job, never expecting to get it. But one afternoon I received a cable, and it was breathtaking. I should shortly be going to South Africa and I informed Benn. He was disappointed but pleased for the honor given me. My association with Benn was excellent. He published a book, *Confessions of a Capitalist,* in which he defended the profit system, wisely, though he didn't understand the first thing about formal economics.

JLR: The first major work you published was *The Theory of Collective Bargaining,* which I consider the greatest book on labor unions. Was there much reaction to it or did it just drop in the ocean?

Hutt: I did my best to arouse controversy. For example, I sent copies to Sidney and Beatrice Webb. I was twice in their mansion near a town called Heyshott. I was invited to visit them by reason of my friendship with a lovely girl called Kitty Dobbs, now Mrs. Malcolm Muggeridge. I knew the Webbs and they knew me. I never got an acknowledgement, not a word, and yet it was an attack on the very basis of what they were doing. You know, Malcolm Muggeridge described Mrs. Webb as "the cruelest woman I ever knew." Kitty had a very poor opinion of the people to whom she introduced me.

JLR: There may not have been much reaction to *The Theory of Collective Bargaining* at the time, but it has since been reprinted two or three times and gotten some attention.

Hutt: It must have had an influence if more and more people have been reading about it, but other critical works have appeared since, like yours.

JLR: One of the things I enjoy about your book is that it is still very readable and you refer to Hawtrey, Jevons, and other economists who were not that far removed chronologically from the period in which you were writing. What is your opinion of Alfred Marshall and his work?

Hutt: He was a decent chap, but very much the dull intellectual. No person who knew him that I have ever met regarded him as a lively figure, or as a person who counted except by reason of the tremendous reputation he enjoyed by being the head of economics teaching at Cambridge.

JLR: Henry Hazlitt said he read Marshall while Hazlitt was young and he did not like Marshall because he was too compromising. In the *Principles* Marshall gives all this pro and con and it's kind of mushy.

Hutt: I think Marshall did intend to write in a manner which would not upset the politicians of his day.

JLR: Your next book was *Economists and*

the Public in 1936. Was that one of your three best if you had to choose?

Hutt: Yes. That was a very fundamental book, as far as I was concerned.

JLR: What was the main message of that book?

Hutt: That the force of competition is not a destructive force. It is exactly the opposite. It is the sole principle of coordination in a complex world in which people with differing objectives and differing tastes can utilize assets and people to satisfy their ends, their objectives.

JLR: Given this view of competition, what about unions?

Hutt: The labor unions today, through their influence upon consumer prices and through their diversion of labor from highly productive to less productive activities, are causing the impoverishment of the masses.

JLR: You believe that is true in America to a serious degree as well as in England?

Hutt: Yes, everywhere. For a short period it is possible for governmental income transfers to hide the reality, insofar as you can tax the owners of the assets which multiply the yields to labor. You can then give more to the relatively poorer classes. And that has been happening. It happened in Britain and has been the cause of British workers falling to about fourth or fifth in the world in income per head.

JLR: I think that a lot of people are aware that the trade unions have seriously harmed the standard of living in the United Kingdom, but are not so aware of it in the United States. The size of the effect will be a little smaller here because they have organized a smaller fraction of the labor force.

Hutt: That is so. But the left constantly displays its sympathy for the underdog and appeals to the best motives of people who do not understand. You can show throughout that the unions are working against the good of the underdog, be it a racial underdog like the blacks or non-whites, or the poor generally, or the immigrants, and so on.

JLR: What about the so-called Harvard school, Richard B. Freeman and James M. Medoff, who argue that unions have positive and negative effects and frequently the positive effects outweigh the negative?

Hutt: That can all be refuted. The general principle about the distribution of income, to which I had been led, is that the magnitude of aggregate income is greatest and its distribution is least unequal when every person employed and the services of every asset are remunerated at the lowest cost necessary to get the services.

JLR: That way of expressing it is correct to economists, but it is very hard to sell that to noneconomists, right?

Hutt: Yes, but the fact that it is very difficult to explain this truth to people, who tend to recoil from it, should not in any way lead us to refrain from observing what we know and stating it in the clearest possible way.

JLR: This raises the issue, as you did in your monograph "Politically Impossible...?," of what role economists should play. That is, to what extent should we compromise the truth for political purposes?

Hutt: As economists, never. But if we feel that we have the power to influence policy in the right sort of way, we can go into politics, in which case our authority as economists is relinquished.

JLR: The Council of Economic Advisors is the worst case, to me, because you are just the paid mouthpiece of the president.

Hutt: Exactly, but of course if you are a paid mouthpiece, you can always resign. If you accept the position with that understanding, I don't see why you could not do good work there. But when I think of Herbert Stein and Martin Feldstein and others, quite able economists technically, I feel that all authority which they could have otherwise commanded is gone because they are obviously trying to...

JLR: Improve the electability of their master, right? Does that contradict your earlier comment about being able to do good work? I guess you have the ear of the president, to some extent.

Hutt: Yes, I often try to think: what would I advise Reagan if I were in a position to advise him? I am pretty sure that I would be saying the same things as now.

JLR: Privately or publically?

Hutt: I don't think I would agree to be an advisor to any person on an understanding that I should be silent on issues which concern the public.

JLR: Let's turn to unions and inflation. Do you believe that the politicians, because of union wage aggression in the United States, try to inflate their way out of unemployment and difficulties in unionized industries? To me, the model really fits the facts in Britain a little more closely.

Hutt: There are considerable differences, but it's still true that labor costs in the unionized industries in the United States are high because productivity is high there and they have been able to force up the price of labor above its competitive level. But, in doing so, they have eradicated a source of demand for all non-competing things—all the rest of industry. It spreads, of course, in the sense that one industry exploits the rest.

JLR: Do you see this in an inflationary context, that it reduces growth in the supply of goods?

Hutt: Yes, it creates a motive for politicians to feel that their monetary authority must inflate. It creates an incentive. I think that the union leaders here in the United States all recognize it.

JLR: You think union leaders are conscious of their inflationary pressures on the politicians?

Hutt: Yes, the union leaders expect to get more benefit out of it than the illusory or purely inflationary rise in demand for their products.

JLR: Let's go back to this issue of recommending wage cuts under some circumstances because this creates price flexibility, otherwise we don't allow the markets to approach market clearing prices and expand employment and output. Martin Bronfenbrenner once said to me in a letter that, in effect, it is unseemly for well-paid professors to suggest wage cuts anywhere because we are well paid and live a comfortable life.

Hutt: The answer would be in the form of another question: Is the fact that professors are well paid, and have a comfortable life, any reason why the possible earning power of the ordinary man in the street should be reduced by 25 percent? That's the point. Leftists don't think in terms of the sufferings of the poor at all, they think in terms of the well-being of the labor leaders. That's how you should reply to Martin Bronfenbrenner.

JLR: Mises, Hayek, and Wicksell seem to emphasize the interest rate and inflationary creation of new loanable funds as the primary boom-bust mechanism. That Austrian type of theory of the inflationary business cycle is somewhat different from your emphasis on pricing defects to explain the existence of depressions, the persistence of them, and to some extent, the nature of the boom.

Hutt: Well, the depression is due to the process of asking too much for the outputs of men and assets.

JLR: Under some conditions, people are not generally asking too much?

Hutt: Yes, but in that case they won't be unemployed. I have explained this is my *Theory of Idle Resources.* Any resource which is unemployed can only be in that condition due to the prices of its services being greater than the community can afford, in the light of the other demands.

JLR: Would you say, then, that all unemployment is voluntary?

Hutt: Yes, it is indeed voluntary, all our unemployment is voluntary.

JLR: Even though you recognize that unions or governmental price-fixing or work rules have priced some people involuntarily out of some sectors of the economy?

Hutt: Yes, of course, but the people who are unemployed. . . may be deliberately refusing employment because they want to be available for an outlet which may yet materialize. That is really a model of full employment.

JLR: Yes, just as active job search is a form of employment.

Hutt: Indeed it is, and it is remunerated by subsequent remuneration.

JLR: What is your basic analysis of the Great Depression? Do you put most emphasis on monetary events, the Smoot-Hawley tariffs, or . . . ?

Hutt: I put all the blame for unutilized resources upon price inflexibility downwards, which includes wage-rate inflexibility downwards.

JLR: Has this price inflexibility worsened over time, primarily due to unions and the welfare state?

Hutt: I think it has. I think the welfare state in many ways encourages people to hold off adjustments in the hope that they will get compensation through the welfare mechanism.

JLR: So not many people moved from Michigan when the auto industry was depressed?

Hutt: Yes, and that robs the community of the stimulus which the first price cuts create, the first time there is a reduction in the price of a thing. You see that happening today in various places in the United States.

JLR: During the recovery?

Hutt: Yes. Certain workers, for example, recently have refused to follow their union, and openly accepted lower wage rates to keep their firm going, to keep the wheels turning. They are benefiting not only themselves but the people from whom they buy—those employed in all the other industries and investing in those industries.

JLR: Is it your general impression that we can show statistically that recessions and depressions were shorter-lived during the nineteenth and early twentieth centuries because prices had to adjust, that is, people couldn't hold out if they wanted to keep eating and they had to price themselves into work more rapidly?

Hutt: Yes, that's probably a factor today. But little bits of news in the press over the past 18 months suggest to me that workers are prepared to accept less than the union wage rates and are prepared to break with their union, indeed, to become scabs, to get employment. That's a very healthy process.

JLR: What about the conflict between the union leaders and the current membership? You're suggesting that the union leaders want to price at such rates that they lose large fractions of their membership, permanently allowing industries like steel to shrink to half or less of their former sizes. What motivates these union leaders to allow such a huge shrinkage in their dues income?

Hutt: They know they are in a dilemma, but they think they can hold out, and somehow things will recover in spite of them not advocating the necessary adjustments. Some of them may be hoping that the workers will not obey the orders they officially have to give. I mean that quite seriously. They rely on the stupidity of the membership.

JLR: Of course, the leaders are running to Washington trying to get subsidies and protections that will allow industries to survive the labor costs that the union leaders have imposed.

Hutt: Yes, but all such methods protect a particular employment in a particular industry to the accompaniment of the extermination of a greater amount of employment elsewhere. And that's why the thing must break down. The source of all employment is the demand from the flow of productive services in one field demanding the flow of productive services in another field.

JLR: One part of your work has dealt with unions and labor-market pricing more generally, and another part concerns the aggregate flow of output, or macroeconomics. My impression is that most labor economists and macroeconomists are not aware of the close connection, but you see these two problems as being closely related.

Hutt: Yes indeed. Macroeconomics is only justified when linked with micro. It's always the pricing mechanism which restores fuller employment, or which brings about greater real income.

JLR: The main pricing issue you look at it the pricing of labor; I don't have the impression that most economists or industrial relations people are aware of this. Is that your impression?

Hutt: It may well be. If so, it accounts for their blind spots on a vital issue. My *Theory of Idle Resources* should really have explained all that.

JLR: As we know, very few books make a big impression and sometimes the ones that do are the wrong ideas.

Hutt: Yes.

JLR: You've spoken eloquently and incisively about the receptivity conditions that are necessary. When your book came out in 1939, that wasn't what people wanted to hear.

Hutt: Quite, exactly.

JLR: In 1982 there was report of a conference in Industrial Relations, which was attended by about 30 of the leading figures in industrial relations research. I would like you to comment on some of the remarks made. For example, the conferees thought that "normal adversarial relationships were healthy."

Hutt: I think it's outrageous. The notion that there should be anything resembling adversarial relations, on any side, in respect of the employment of assets and the employment of the labor that works with the assets is, it seems to me, almost unbelievable. It needn't be. You have the market to assist you and the market depends on competition. And competition is only the substitution of a lower cost method of achieving any objective, whether it is material or nonmaterial, up to the point at which other objectives become more important, that is, when costs exceed predicted or expected price. There can be no exceptions to this type of analysis.

JLR: But these were the leading figures in industrial relations.

Hutt: I know, but the leading figures in industrial relations are complete fools because they have not studied all the rational thought which has gone on in order to consider these issues.

JLR: The report said that they identified with "free collective bargaining among equals," and that they wished to help the "underdog," which is why they devoted most of their attention to the union side.

Hutt: If they really want to help the underdog, then the first thing they have to do is to realize the quite general economic principle that the distribution of income is rendered most equal, or least unequal, when every person is offered his job at the least necessary to get his services, in the same way that assets are employed when they are offered the least necessary to get their services.

JLR: And this makes the aggregate yield higher?

Hutt: Yes, indeed. We must find some way to persuade the rank and file in industry to accept such low wage rates that they are fully employed, and on a sufficiently wide scale, so that each cut in the price of the product creates demand for the noncompeting products of other activities. But you can't get past that problem without dragging in Say's law.

JLR: The conferees thought that "wage uniformity was one of collective bargaining's greatest accomplishments" and they viewed "with considerable dismay the increasingly chaotic nature of wage relationships."

Hutt: Any wage uniformity which is not the consequence of market freedom and the chance that the productivity of the different individuals remunerated is more or less identical is counterproductive. If you paid everybody the same amount, irrespective of their contribution, you would destroy all incentive to improvement.

JLR: On the political front, the conference report said that "the unions push for broad sets of objectives in the interest of workers and society generally."

Hutt: The interest of one set of workers and the interest of other workers are always violently opposed if it is a question of paying the one more than the market rate. If anyone is paid the market rate, then he can be harmed by somebody else insisting upon being paid more than the market rate because his employment is threatened, or at least his continuous employment. He may not lose his job, but somebody else will.

JLR: And in his capacity as a consumer?

Hutt: Yes, in that role also. It is equally vital. Everything I say concerning an individual's earning power is paralleled by the power of the individual in society who loses when costs in any industry are raised, including labor costs.

JLR: The report concluded with a statement of "continuing faith in the efficacy of collective bargaining as the cornerstone of the American industrial relations system" and that "our economic and social problems can best be resolved through tripartite union-management-government discussion and collaboration."

Hutt: Nobody has argued more strongly than I have that if labor wishes—the representatives of labor, on behalf of those they represent—to make the fundamental managerial decisions, then they must become fundamental entrepreneurs, which they can do by paying interest to labor plus profits minus losses. Then the whole of those profits and losses are borne by the workers who can best rent the assets. Theoretically, that is possible. That means, in fact, a solution is possible for those who believe that there is a problem.

JLR: Why don't we see that more commonly?

Hutt: I think that the Mondales, the Harts, and the O'Neills stand in the way.

JLR: Really? Which means what?

Hutt: If the workers wanted to undertake entrepreneurship, they could do so by sharing it—which I recommended in my 1982 *Policy Review* article—or by taking it outright. They would have to borrow the funds from their union or somewhere else, and buy out the whole company, all of its assets, and appoint their own managers, or appoint the same ones, then run it under their direction so as to maximize the aggregate yield so that the workers would get more than their rate of interest on what they put in.

JLR: Something like one-third of the value of equity stocks are worker pension funds and the same is true for bonds, so it's pretty clear that with very few changes, workers would do this. Isn't the problem that a firm is such a dynamic problem that you couldn't have shared entrepreneurship? Maybe workers don't want to tie up their wealth in such a narrow form?

Hutt: They could still sell their share and each individual worker could sell his job and his share of the capital to anybody outside. That's obvious. But I didn't put that forward, and I made that clear, as a practical suggestion. I simply wanted to show the absurdity of the grouse that the workers have got no alternative. We've already got the institutions for labor participation. The workers have always had that and apparently not wanted it, and I don't blame them.

JLR: So *laissez faire* is open to all organizational forms, but not all forms are viable or competitive.

Hutt: Exactly.

JLR: *The Economics of the Colour Bar*—it came out in 1964—was that your first systematic treatment of the discrimination problem and the color bar laws?

Hutt: The first adequate treatment of my type of view. We had a lot of liberals in my country, quite sincere and genuine, who viewed my opinions as anathema. But I wanted to build from the bottom up. I wanted the poor people to come up, and to get opportunities. They should be refused no employment opportunities which were ever available to them, no matter what harm their accepting employment might cause for people better off than they are. And that was hopeless; that was viewed as a wicked ploy in the interest of the capitalist. Certainly the capitalists will always benefit under a better system.

JLR: Just as everyone else does.
Hutt: Exactly.

JLR: I was curious about why you did not cite Gary Becker's *Economics of Discrimination.* You were probably aware of it.

Hutt: I did not see any way in which reference to it would improve my exposition without making it very, very long. To bring in the Gary Becker argument and to put it in its correct perspective would have taken a full chapter. In fact I had a rather long chapter originally and I shortened it instinctively, I believe.

JLR: Becker's book never satisfactorily answers how the discriminatory consequences of racial preferences can persist in markets, yet he wants this result to persist. I saw the two books as being at odds to some degree.

Hutt: Yes, I agree with you.

JLR: Professor Hutt, are there any issues you want to raise?

Hutt: I simply want to say this: as soon as I entered into academic life, I saw that the fixing of the price of labor under coercion, whether it occurs through private organizations like a labor union or the coercion of the state in the interest of the same people, could not possibly bring about a state of affairs that any humane student could accept with equanimity. The present system is impoverishing, not only in material terms but even worse, in human terms. There will be plenty of effort to upset your reasoning, if you try to put this point of view over—from Harvard, from the Medoffs and Freemans, and from other pragmatists who counsel the appeasement of organized labor. Today, managements, on the whole, believe that such appeasement is enlightenment, instead of fighting on behalf of the underdog, firstly, as consumer and secondly, as an employee who can contribute to the common pool, not only in that particular entrepreneur's field, but also in all the noncompeting fields.

JLR: Doesn't that trace back to the intellectuals? The only reason managers don't think highly of their legitimate function in resisting union aggression is that intellectuals have sold this idea for over a century.

Hutt: Yes, indeed they have. Of course, insofar as they have done that through politics, they have done it in the interest of their own advancement. And they have got the clergy on their side. Very easy to do.

JLR: The clergy is almost beyond education in economic analysis.

Hutt: Yes, but you've got a lovely opportunity here. Why should the religious leaders always side with poverty? With the causes of poverty? Is it because they really believe that impoverishing the underdog will assist him?

JLR: How would you answer a scholar who says that we have had as rapid an economic advance in the era of large unions and the welfare state as we had during the nineteenth century?

Hutt: The advancement certainly has been continuous. The defenders of poverty creation will never be able to show by statistical studies that, correlated with the growth of so-called liberal institutions, the workers as a whole have benefited from unionization, that is, that their real incomes have risen as much as otherwise would have occurred. The effect of competition among workers in different fields, if it had been unrestrained, would have led to far more people in the higher paid kinds of work and far fewer in the lower paid kinds of work.

JLR: You have had a long career. What is your feeling about the drift of academic opinion now?

Hutt: I often think about that. In my more optimistic moods, I am very optimistic. I think of what a flourishing group the Philadelphia Society is, for example, and I think of the Mont Pelerin Society, an international organization, of which I was a founding member. That is all very promising. But take Britain. It is an appalling example of a country ruined by the radicals. Before World War II, she was easily ranked second in the world in terms of the average standard of living, but now ranks way down the list. That is not due to war damage. It is due entirely to the wage structure.

JLR: It's not only wages. It's the aggressiveness, the hostility, the adversarial mentality, and the work rules which discourage investment.

Hutt: Yes, indeed, that's one of its manifestations. All those restraints have been introduced as a method of keeping control of the price of labor. The short run belief is that strike threats and similar devices enable the worker to get more. Of course you can get more for a particular group—always. But always at the expense of the rest of the workers and very largely at the expense of the consumers, and that's not being perceived in Britain. Lord Harris of the Institute of Economic Affairs, Lord Bauer, Basil Yamey, and a large number of others who are very highly regarded in Britain—their viewpoints, which, I believe, coincide with mine, are heard by Mrs. Thatcher and her government, although, for reasons which we can all perceive, she can't do much to rectify things. Poor Mrs. Thatcher. If she moves the way she should, she's out. There will be a revolt on the part of the House of Commons and the various members of Parliament. All parties depend upon special interest groups, which have reduced democracy to an absurdity. I think she understands that position, but she doesn't seem to be in a position to say so, effectively.

JLR: So you're optimistic in terms of the intellectual and academic changes you're seeing, but there is little short-term political hope?

Hutt: I don't know enough about the day-to-day political realities to be able to suggest how they can be overcome. But if you have an indoctrinated electorate, how can you educate them? Or disindoctrinate them? They are almost as much slaves of old ideas as the Soviets are.

JLR: What is your explanation for the part of labor economics dealing with unions and collective bargaining being sliced off from the mainstream of economics, thereby being freed from what you described as rational analysis?

Hutt: It is terrible. That is a field in which there ought to be crystal clarity about the relations of the price of labor and the price of the services of assets to the flow of productive services, and the degree to which the assets and the people are fully employed. Those were problems that demanded solution, but what are you getting from the older universities in the United States?

JLR: How can people be so soft-headed intellectually? Maybe there is no explanation for the bulk of intellectual/academic work being so poor, of such poor quality.

Hutt: Yes, yes, and so often dressed up in high-falutin' terms.

JLR: You have thought a lot about the issue of constitutionality. You wrote a constitution, in effect, for South Africa, about how to gradually get out of this box. It's obvious that you can't have immediate one-man, one-vote or you'll have the same regression experienced in the rest of black Africa, just as conservatives talked about if they had immediate independence from colonial powers.

Hutt: Yes, South Africa's critics recognize that, but nobody is putting the point over. When I finish the work I am on now, I might get down to another attack on apartheid and try to defend my country, although I've got to defend it by saying that I think apartheid is an abominable policy.

JLR: You made this terrific point in *Economics of the Colour Bar* about all the passes and checks in South Africa: it's exactly like in the Soviet Union, which the government denounces so vigorously. Collectivism is collectivism. You mentioned the work of Buchanan and Tullock on the constitutional issue. How do you get out of this box?

Hutt: I don't know. If I ever get down to that, the first thing I'd do is tackle the work of Tullock and Buchanan, to make the obvious point.

JLR: Thank you, Professor Hutt.

Reprinted with permission of the *Journal of Labor Research*

A FOREWORD TO
W.H. HUTT'S PRINCIPLE
OF SOCIAL JUSTICE

by
Connie Moran Kirkpatrick

Few economists, and certainly no politicians, dare label the strike or strike-threat
practices of unionized labor as a "coercive
power of extortion" that "impoverishes the
relatively poor and enriches the relatively
affluent." The argument does not click
with what the general electorate has been
conditioned to hail as a demonstration for
workers' rights in the name of "social justice." Many snub the dusty objections of
the classical theorists to such non-market
contrivances of labor scarcity, as such reasoning is unsuitable for how *they* perceive
the modern imbalances among owners,
managers and workers of a firm. Adher-
ence to classical principles—when applied
dyslogistically to criticize labor's "right to
strike"—is considered unfashionable, even
gauche, and thus rejected, for it threatens
one's desired self-image as harboring "liberal" attitudes—meant here, ironically

enough, largely in the classical sense. Yet not to recognize the strike system for the sham that it is, is to succumb to intellectual cowardice.

The following essay is contained as a chapter in the forthcoming book, *Labor's Disadvantage*, by William H. Hutt. Drawing upon previous writings by other classical economists, the author succeeds in elevating the labor-strike controversy from its rhetorical gutter and bringing it back to economics. Specifically, he exposes the unfortunate confusion held by many that the interests of management and workers are inherently opposed, and that the labor strike system is synonymous with the pursuit of egalitarianism.

Quite to the contrary, the consequences of union practices are shown to be deplorably regressive, for the privileged union members achieve short-term economic gains largely at the expense of those who are continually confined to suboptimal occupations.

Yet because this vision of reality is blurred, irrationality prevails. For example, although the working conditions and remuneration of workers in many occupations have certainly come a long way since the days of *Das Kapital*, many union workers today still are only too eager to credit the unions, rather than technological advancement for this progress. Small wonder, then, that many workers stand ready to toss a wrench in the works in the line of union strategy.

In contrast to this dupery, Hutt defends the merits of the truly egalitarian "consumer-vote" system, whereby everyone, through his consumer role, influences the productive process. In conjunction with an untrammeled labor market, this system of "consumer sovereignty" ensures the most efficient, productive placement of assets and labor, which in turn raises the aggregate level of income for labor and narrows the disparities among existing incomes. It is only within the realm of free markets, therefore, that the term "social justice" bears any real significance.

To an economist, many of the basic premises presented in the essay will sound familiar. Still, even if one disagrees with them, one has to be careful. The author welcomes the challenge.

THE PRINCIPLE OF SOCIAL JUSTICE

by
W. H. Hutt

To expose the apparent, almost universal cynicism in government policies affecting organized labor in no arduous task. Such labor policies claim to be fighting for "social justice." Yet nearly everywhere their effect is to depress the economic scale of those workers whose marginal productivity falls short of wage-rates forced above market-clearing values. The only "merit" of such policies may indeed be that they create a purpose for a politically vendible antipoverty program!

The hypocrisy of it all is clear. William Simon, former Secretary of the Treasury in the United States, reveals that, for instance, hypocrisy is so common among Congressmen and officials that it is taken for granted—as "play-acting at moral outrage." The late Hubert Humphrey was an outstanding example. Simon reports that he and Humphrey were

good friends, and he knew quite well that I was no more "inhumane" than he. He got a prankish pleasure, however, out of

*denouncing me publicly during the New
York crisis. On one occasion, when I was
testifying before the Joint Economic
Committee on the possible financial impact of default, Hubert put on a remarkable show. As the cameras rolled, he
peered down at me grimly and ranted
away about my "inhumanity"—and then,
as the cameras swung away from him to
capture my reaction, Hubert winked!*

*Another time, after denouncing me
again in rolling rhetoric, he rose, magnifi-
cent in his wrath, and, arms waving,
glasses sliding down to the tip of his
nose, thundered, "Yes—and Arthur
Burns will say, 'Part the waters!' and he
will rescue all the Big Banks. And eight
million little people will go down the
drain." When the TV cameras were gone
and the hearing was over, Hubert placed
his arm heavily about my shoulders and
said, "Bill, that came from my heart." I
answered dryly, "It certainly didn't come
from your head." And Hubert chuckled
appreciatively. Politics required that he
portray me as a monster, and he assumed
that I would understand. Unfortunately I
did. Hubert is a warm-hearted man who,
like most liberals, is virtually illiterate in
economics.*[1]

Both in action, and in passivity in the
face of defiant and quite cynical coercion
by unions, governments have managed to

create an image of themselves as motivated by the highest egalitarian ideals, and with sincere concern for all endeavors to achieve a better well-being for the people. And the unions naturally uphold a parallel line. Mr. Peregrine Worsthorne explains that the British unions' "spectacularly provocative" and "literally awe-inspiring . . . disregard for public approval" is due chiefly to an "authority" which they have acquired through having somehow won acceptance for a " . . . commanding idea that has become, in recent years, invincible: the idea of social justice."[2]

When unions strike today, they claim to be struggling for "social justice." Moreover, over the last century this or a similar battle cry has induced almost universal public support for the "moderate" use of strike-threat power. Mainly because fights by unions are considered by the people as a whole to be against injustices, it often seems irrelevant whether the weapons for disruption of the productive process are either strikes and boycotts, or physical intimidation, sabotage, arson, bribery of politicians and so forth.

Although violent and unsavory methods of coercion are normally kept in the background, union negotiators let it be known that they are prepared to use these weapons. Thus, when governmental powers are not used to establish "social justice" as the unions conceive of it, and when "peaceful" disruption via the concerted withdrawal of labor seems unlikely to inflict sufficient damage on stockholders—usually because there are too many potential interlopers from suboptimal occupations—then the unions feel justified in organizing and financing their own crusade of physical coercion. Sometimes, these powers are ruthlessly employed. That non-strikers or non-combatants may be injured or ruined is no concern of the unions while they are fighting for social justice. Their methods are sacrosanct because the end is.

Union spokesmen write at times as though they believe that, in a free market, "the capitalists" have the power to determine both the workers' remuneration and conditions of work unilaterally. If that had been so, the powers that governments have conceded to the unions might appear to have provided the required correction. But the conviction is wrong. Certainly managements have the legal right, on behalf of the residual claimants, to make wage offers. Nevertheless, in a free market, managements have no power to influence the level of wage-rates to their advantage, any more than they have power to influence either the prices which it will be to their advantage to ask, or the corresponding outputs which they judge it will be profitable to produce.

Entrepreneurial discretion, therefore, is subject to a social discipline, under which costs and prices are determined. The coercive power of collusion within the labor camp can be observed, on the other hand, as aimed at forcing managements to ignore this disciplined market process. Viewed as such, the entrepreneurs are labor's adversaries, but only in the sense that any person forced at gunpoint to part with his property is an adversary.

The full power of the union, says Worsthorne, "in any advanced technological society is almost limitless." And there is no "countervailing spirit of comparable aggressive purposefulness animating the other side of industry."[3] However, the "power" of the unions is derived from its privileges. Hence the vital question can be raised: because society has indeed today entrusted "*almost* limitless" privileges to private, sectional interests, has it not a duty at least to curb or limit those privileges when they are obviously being abused? Indeed, ought not society withdraw *all* special dispensations or favors when the unions exercise those privileges irresponsibly?

Still, nobody ever negatively replies to the unions' indignant demands with equal bluntness, because, comments Mr. Worsthorne, "However immoral some of the methods used by the trade unions are felt to be, their basic aim—improving the lot of the working people—is still felt to be of almost religious significance."[4]

Obviously the crucial question is whether the unions' fight is, in practice, for "justice" or, indeed, ever has been. Would it not be more accurate to say that the unions are, as Lord Feather admitted in 1975, fighting solely in the prospective interests of their own members? Do defenders of union methods really believe that reliance on force is conducive to the "just" division of the value of production? Have the unions or other defenders of the strike-threat system ever produced a rigorous attempt to show this? If such an attempt had been found, it would be quoted here. Has the idea ever occurred to labor's spokesmen that their gains have been won, not mainly from stockholders and the rich, but rather from consumers, workers and providers of wage-multiplying assets in noncompeting fields, including the nonunionized sector, and those whom can be termed "the neglected victims," often confined to suboptimal activities?

In an imaginary system in which private coercion in every form is effectively forbidden, however, the terms of the wage contract offered would be determined on the one side by the entrepreneur's judgement of the marginal prospective yield to investment (a) in the assets needed to employ labor, and (b) in the particular labor inputs which individual workers are predicted to be able to provide with "profit," that is, at the prevailing per unit price for output dictated by the market. The acceptance of the contract offered would be determined, in turn, in light of the workers' judgement of their alternative modes of employment. Where, exactly, does the alleged "disadvantage" come into play in this method? Is there any cause for misgivings at all? Again, at what point and how is the worker exploited?

In Chapter Five of his *New Studies,* entitled "The Atavism of Social Justice," F.A. Hayek shows that, as ordinarily used, the concept of " 'social justice'... has no meaning whatever" in a truly free society; although it has for nearly "a century dominated political discussion, and has everywhere been successfully used to advance claims of particular groups for a larger share in the good things of life." The very concept is, he writes, "intellectually disreputable—nothing more than an empty formula, conventionally used to assert that a particular claim is justified without giving any reason."[5]

Hayek does not cast doubt upon the usefulness of the concept of "justice" in social relations. On the contrary, he insists that "rules of just individual conduct are as indispensable to the preservation of a society of free men as endeavors to realize 'social' justice are incompatible with it,"[6] a proposition which he had enunciated in the second volume of his *magnum opus, Law, Legislation and Liberty*.

What people seem to mean by the term "social justice" is, says Hayek, "what used to be called 'distributive justice'." The word "justice," he continues, "has meaning only as a rule of human conduct . . . it can have no application to the results of a market economy: there can be no distributive justice where no one distributes."[7]

The argument is both subtle and profound. It can be expressed alternatively, however, as follows. The market system is as impersonal as the Straits of Gibralter, a book of logarithms, a pharmacopia, or a bulldozer. In a free market, prices, and hence individual incomes, are determined through the interaction of millions of preferences, judgments and actions. Even when these prices are changed by deliberate individual or group action, for private or sectional advantage, the market system itself remains neutral—a mere tool, like a spanner or a slide-rule, incapable of acting immorally or anti-socially. And even if, in theory at any rate, either the expression of human preferences or the response to those preferences could occur only through collective action—through some form of political voting—the objectives can still be attained through the market, which seeks out the people and the assets required.

The phrase "social justice" is commonly used to imply criticism either of market influences or of private, i.e., nonmarket influences (whether expressed individually or through government). It suggests that people are underpaid. But however woolly the notion is in the mind of the majority who use it, it can have meaning when one considers the world as it is. Actual prices may reflect "contrived scarcities" (implying monopolistic abuse), and so there will be some grounds for calling those prices "unjust." Yet, when prices (and hence incomes) are wholly market-determined, the present author has always referred to them as representing "natural" scarcities, to distinguish them from man-made or "contrived," nonmarket scarcities or prices. And because the latter are manmade, it seems that the medieval notion of the just price may not always have been entirely void of meaning. In fact, Hayek himself enunciates, very briefly, what we regard and describe as "the true principle of social justice," a concept which if it were understood could be universally accepted as such.

The principle that Hayek puts forward is, he perceives, connected with the notion of justice in remuneration of assets as well as workers—an approach that is adopted

here. The determination of labor's remuneration is "just," according to Hayek,
when it "contributes as much as possible
to increasing the chances of any member of
the community picked out at random...
(to) find (his) most effective place in the
overall pattern of activities—the place in
which (he is) likely to make the greatest
contribution to aggregate output."[8]

Moreover, the market system is not "au-
tomatic," but run by people in their entrepreneurial role. As entrepreneurs, people
accept responsibility for their decisions by
bearing the risk of being penalized for error and rewarded for success. In Hayek's
words, it is "a game of skill as well as a
game of chance. Above all, it is a game
which serves to elicit from each player the
highest worthwhile contribution to the
common pool from which each will win an
uncertain share." These beneficial results
accrue, Hayek explains, through the
spreading of the information needed for co-
ordination.

The information of which Hayek is
speaking takes the form of prices—
"market signals" which tell the producer
"what to produce and what means to use in
producing it...(and) ensure that all of a
society's dispersed knowledge will be taken
into account and used." But the virtues of
the system are realized "only if the prices
he (the producer) can get are determined

solely by market forces and not by the coercive powers of government."[10] Unfortunately, rather than allow prices to "be free to tell the truth,"[11] in this century, says Hayek, governments increasingly have falsified "the market price signals" to give "benefits to groups claimed to be particularly deserving."[12] Most people do not realize that the aggregate income, which they believe can be redistributed, is available, "only *because* returns for the different efforts are held out by the market with little regard to deserts or needs," not perceiving that the "possessors of large incomes" have acquired those incomes "from continual redisposition of resources."[13]

The development of Hayek's reasoning and conclusions presented here emphasizes the inegalitarian effects of all nonmarket prices. We propose to support the thesis that market prices themselves exert egalitarian pressures, which, if protected by law and administration, not only maximize the material well-being of the poorer classes, but also extend the greatest scope for the achievement of nonmaterial objectives on the part of all.

In reality, however, as Hayek points out, demands are made "under the name of 'social justice' which assert a moral claim on government that it give us what it can take by force from those who . . . have been more successful than the rest of society. Such an artificial alteration of the relative attractiveness of the different directions of productive efforts can only be counterproductive."[14] He further suggests that under such a market system, those at the lower end of the income scale, actually reap more than they would in a centrally directed system.[15]

Society applies a double standard, however, to prices other than wage-rates. For example, it is almost universally accepted as just, and for the general good of the whole community, when all products are purchased in the cheapest market. Indeed, in the case of government contracts, failure to follow this simple rule is, in most circumstances, regarded as evidence of corruption. If the lowest bid is not accepted, an explanation is demanded.[16] Why, then, should not the same principle apply in the community's purchase of labor services?

In light of the above considerations, it must be emphasized again what, we suggest, is "the true principle of social justice," which is as follows: *Social justice is achieved when the flow of wages is maximized and the degree of inequality in that flow is minimized; and this will occur when, in the absence of monopsonistic exploitation, and in each occupation, the offer of remuneration to every worker is at the minimum judged necessary to attract and retain his services from alternative opportunities.*[17]

Exactly the same process determines social justice in the remuneration of the services of assets. Justice is achieved and aggregate income from ownership of the community's aggregate assets is maximized when entrepreneurs are free to purchase assets of given attributes (or the services of assets) at the minimum prices needed to attain them. This same process tends also to maximize residues and minimize deficiencies, thereby benefiting the entrepreneur.

If a policy which consciously aims at seeking social justice as interpreted here is accepted, how would it affect relative yields to property and risk-taking on the one side and to efforts and skills on the other? Organized labor can be expected to reply that such a policy will award managements the long-awaited power to force down the remuneration of labor to starvation levels. The true effect is very different.

First, the nearer the prices of the services of labor and assets approximate their market-clearing values as a result of free market pressures, the greater will be the pie to be divided. *Ceteris paribus,* increased competition among suppliers will certainly reduce the earnings of labor and assets in a firm or occupation, especially when demand for the product is inelastic. But for every individual downward cost adjustment the entrepreneur achieves, he tends to reduce the magnitude of similar adjustments needed to maximize real income and create full employment in other, non-competing occupations and industries. We are, of course, returning to a consideration of the implications of Say's law. The result is that, other things being equal, all pricing which raises profitable sales causes a dynamic addition to aggregate real income, which constitutes in turn the source of all demands.

Second, the nearer competition forces down wage-rates towards market-clearing levels (where they have previously exceeded those levels), and hence pushes up wage-rates in other occupations, the greater will be the rise in labor's aggregate absolute income. The proportion accruing to labor, however, will be less in conseqence. That is, the workers may receive a greater aggregate income, although a reduced proportion of a larger total. The theoretical justification for this simple statement can be found in the book, *The Strike-Threat System*, in the following slightly amended passage:

> *All economizing displacements, considered in isolation, tend to reduce the percentage share of those whose assets or labor provide the services economized. For example, every time unskilled or unprivileged workers manage to sneak through the fences and work their way*

into a skilled or privileged occupation, their entry tends, ceteris paribus, to reduce the relative share of labor in any activity affected... (Furthermore,) any economization of labor expresses an increased demand for the services of the complimentary assets, such as capital used, just as any economization of such assets expresses an increased demand for the services of the labor used. Each economy tends therefore to raise the opposite party's relative share.

Exactly the same principle is relevant with diseconomies (such as an earthquake, terrorist activity, or the raising of a wage-rate by a strike threat, or collusively enforced output restraint). The reduced contribution of a factor will mean a raise in its percentage share in the reduced value of the output. The general principle can be stated as follows.

Given unchanged knowledge, the application of further increments of any factor of production to a fixed "amount" of any other factor of production, or to a fixed "amount" of any unchanging combination of other production factors will, in the absence of any economies of scale, yield less than proportionate average returns. Thus, a reduction in the number of man-hours worked,[18] the volume of complementary assets being assumed un-

changed in magnitude and composition, must mean a rise in labor's share. A growth in the stock of assets in an industry, with the number of man-hours unresponsive, must have a similar effect. To put it differently, if the quantity of services rendered by any factor of production rises or falls relative to an assumed fixed quantity of services which owners of complementary factors of production find it profitable to retain or bring into a particular activity, the proportion of the value of the product which accrues to those who provide relatively larger or smaller inputs will fall or rise respectively.[19]

Yet it is the lowest income groups who will reap the greatest benefits from a general freeing of the labor market. As soon as society can adjust to a regime in which wage-rate barriers to upward mobility have been dissolved, a conspicuous rise in the real earning power of the poorest classes will follow. For such a price policy implies not only the maximum aggregate product of labor, but also the maximum equality in the distribution of its value.

As stressed above, our "principle of social justice" has the same relevance to entrepreneurial remuneration, which is itself a residue. The risk-takers' services are provided by people, not by assets; and "profits" have to be recognized as subject to an identical rule.[20] "Profits" earned are a form of "payment by results," and "profits" are always reduced by competition—through entrepreneurial fears of augmented supplies of output of a firm's rivals. The reader is reminded of our definition of "competition" as the process of substituting lower cost methods of producing and marketing any commodity or service, in response to the power of consumers to devote their income to preferred or lower cost commodities.

The acceptance of social justice as conceived here as the aim of labor policy would mean a complete reversal of present attitudes and actions towards workers in the unionized sector. Every wage-rate forced above free-market levels by coercion consigns wage-earners to suboptimal occupations via lay-off or exclusion. All along, barriers like the enforcement of the so-called "equal pay for equal work" rule have been denying the underprivileged the right to bid against protected incumbents. And the removal of such barriers would eradicate immediately the dominant avoidable cause of the present degree of inequality of incomes. Better remunerated and more productive employment outlets would become available as rapidly as the adjustments required could occur.

The union-dictated "rate for the job" not only shuts off access to the bargaining table for the initially less well-qualified or "non-preferred" workers; it also contributes to closing entry to a trade or profession—the spirit of which is most clearly manifest through licensing requirements. Egalitarians who apprehend these consequences will always welcome the elimination of wage-rate restraints.[21]

The substitution of just and fair relationships would, then, mean the removal of all these barriers and make possible the proclamation of what should be every individual's most basic, and constitutionally entrenched human right, namely, that of contributing freely to the common pool of output where he believes his productivity will be highest, that is, where society is prepared and forced to pay more for his services than he is at present earning.

While some readers may suspect us of neglecting the downward pressure on returns to workers in the high-paid categories, our "rule of social justice" nevertheless explicitly includes the phrase, "irrespective of any adverse consequences which formerly privileged workers must expect." Most important is that the cheapening of the product of relatively high skills affords to the consumer an increase in real income, thus enhancing demand for the services of men and assets in the noncompeting activities, as well as in the high-skill activities. Moreover, the main principle is reemphasized in that downward pressure on the earned incomes of the privileged would be concrete proof of the egalitarian nature of the market system. Still, however, the burden on the more efficient workers is likely to be relatively low in most cases.

Justice in income distribution is not simply synonymous with equality in income distribution. Even if ideal equality of opportunity could be achieved, the free market would still demonstrate the necessity to offer very high salaries in order to secure, say, a sufficient quantity and quality of surgeons' services.[22] But greater individual freedom, which ensures greater equality of opportunity, is certainly conducive to greater equality of condition and income.

It is, however, far more difficult for economists today to communicate egalitarian ideas effectively than it was for Adam Smith and his successors to expose the follies of mercantilism in the eighteenth century. Powerful stereotypes dominate the minds of opnion-makers and electors. Many have been conditioned to believe that all classes of the poor can benefit from a system under which all special interests in low income circles are favored.

This is of course, the old fallacy of composition. Each profession or occupation which can protect itself and raise its income by prohibiting other men and other assets from supplying additional inputs and outputs in its privileged fields should, it is widely held, be encouraged to do so. Any occupation harmed by the process, should organize and raise *its* earnings in the same way. Not recognizing that all protection from competition is "exploitation" of the remainder of society, opinion-makers and opinion-acceptors actually seem to believe that the universal exploitation of all can be for the good of all. Such a belief is the gravest fallacy. It has condemned and still condemns vast numbers to relative impoverishment.

Occupational protectionism impoverishes simply because it *is* protectionism. It closes the door to those who could otherwise make their largest contribution to income in the originally privileged occupations and hence the initially best-paid occupations. Admittedly, there are some occupations in which consumers may need special protection from the unqualified. But the certification system can all too easily degenerate into mere restriction of entry. In general, independent certification provides efficient consumer protection. What is *necessary* is genuine equality of opportunity to qualify. And when that has been achieved, relative wage-rates will be influenced by the relative scarcity of the inborn skills and the acquired powers of those certified.

The powerful egalitarian effect of what we have called "the free-market determination of income" can be further demonstrated. If all persons had the right of free access to every bargaining table and the untrammeled right to accept any job at any remuneration offered by management—regardless of how much their employment might harm privileged workers—the interlopers would never choose to move from occupations of relatively high remuneration and productivity to occupations of relatively low incomes and productivity. Rather they would always try to move in the opposite direction, thereby inducing an enormous exodus from suboptimal towards optimal occupations. One could expect indeed that official pressure, recognizing the objective, would assist the required mobility in every possible way. The frequency distribution of incomes would therefore become biased towards higher incomes.

This desired result would be most successfully accomplished, we must repeat, when every potential supplier of labor was completely free to accept any job which any entrepreneur offered him, on terms that could (in the absence of fraud or misrepresentation) attract him away from alternative avenues for his services. And the rule applies, we must reiterate, irrespective of any adverse consequences which formerly privileged workers must accept.

Not only would the facilitation of "upward mobility" to more productive kinds of work be a major egalitarian factor, it would cause relative scarcity in the supply of "put and carry" kinds of work, and hence of real earnings in them. In addition, in a society which is enlightened enough to plan policy in the light of our "social justice principle," direct positive action to ease the costs of the upward trend—particularly in the form of education and inculcation of basic skills—would be a factor.

It follows that the poorer classes will always benefit most from the success of any policy which aims at social justice in our sense. The method is, the reader should never forget, that of *ensuring that all kinds of labor shall be remunerated at the lowest wage-rates or salaries needed to acquire and retain those workers who can be profitably employed.*

Moreover, in any industry, a rise in the aggregate yield to ownership of property is always conducive to a parallel rise in the aggregate yield to labor. The prosperity of an enterprise tends to cause its expansion, thereby enhancing demand for labor. But where additions to the assets stock stand in a competing rather than a complementary relationship to labor—that is, a competitor in the same productive process increases his stock of capital and/or labor—the workers' percentage share must, of course, fall, but only as a proportion of aggregate income. The absolute volume of wages and salaries would be almost certain to rise. Hence, the interests of the complementary parties—i.e., among owners, workers and managers in the same firm—are not likely to diverge in practice. Yet is it not clear that, when organized workers fight against the adoption of labor-economizing managerial arrangements or equipment in their industry, they do so for the same reasons that they try to prevent less-favored workers from sharing in their privileges? All possible advantages enjoyed by organized workers who succeed in forcing the abandonment of potential economies appear to us to be so obviously anti-social that it is really quite remarkable how society has tolerated for so long their legal right to restrain technological progress.

Summarizing, though the proportion of labor's remuneration in aggregate income may fall slightly during a period in which the competition of labor-saving assets is generally growing, the absolute level of labor's remuneration is far more likely to rise than fall as a result. This successful "economizing-displacement," enabling a given piece of work to be done by fewer workers or through assets of a reduced value, has been primarily responsible for the continuous augmentation over the centuries of the real value of "employment outlets." The prodigious rise in the real value of the services of men must be attributed to the cumulative effects of multitudinous labor-saving devices in reducing costs and prices. For in so doing it has been raising demands, not only for non-competing consumer goods and services, but for non-competing productive assets and services as a whole, including labor. The adoption of a system based on frank recognition of our "social justice principle" would, in its practical consequences, enormously raise the earnings of women, juveniles and (in the United States) of most Blacks, Mexican-Americans, and those of Indian ancestry. In the absence of any relaxation of immigration restraints, the price of unskilled labor would rise conspicuously relative to the price of skilled labor, through its sheer scarcity. In the United States, for example, the present average earnings per head of unskilled, non-unionized workers would increase, and the average earnings per head of those in the skilled and unionized sector could *possibly* fall. This is because the numbers of workers allowed to enter the more highly-paid and more productive occupations would increase sharply.

We have used the word "possibly" because if we ignore conceivable, but not safely predictable, dynamic reactions, absolute wage-rates per head in highly-paid occupations would not necessarily fall. A rapid increase in real income would, indeed, be likely to raise real demands for the products of the more highly-paid artisans proportionally or even, possibly, more than proportionally. There could be a "leveling-up" rather than a "leveling-down."

If the above reasoning is sound, it means that ultimately politics under the anti-democratic principle of "one man, one vote," has had the opposite consequences of what electorates have believed themselves to have been supporting. Majorities, having greater total political power than minorities, might have been expected rationally to seek the removal of barriers and hence acquire a maximum income for themselves. But one finds exactly the opposite in actual achievements. Impoverishing policies have been encouraged, not frustrated, while the powerful equalizing tendencies of free-market pressures have been held off. Thus, we have been forced to our rather shocking conclusion that *reliance on the coercive strike or strike-threat, since the very earliest days of unionism, has been all along impoverishing the relatively poor and enriching the relatively affluent.* Yet the ostensible purpose has throughout been to reduce, not exacerbate, income inequalities in the market-value determination of incomes.[23]

The unions have without doubt raised the incomes of certain privileged minorities. The words "privileged minorities" are justified. Let us remember, for instance, that in the United States, little more than one-fifth of non-farm workers are union members, while the proportion of union members to non-union workers has been shrinking for some time. Indeed, the sole reason for the survival of the use of coercive power in attempts to raise the remuneration of strikers is the fact that this method has often won them considerable gains, not so much against investors in the firms in which they are employed (as a supposed rectification of "labor's disadvantage in bargaining") but mainly at the expense of consumers, non-competing producers, and the "neglected victims" generally.

Nowhere is this truth so patent as in the use of the strike-threat method by public employee unions. In such cases, it is the taxpayers (that is, consumers of the state's services) who are clearly discernible as the exploited class. The usual claim that the strikers are seeking part of the "profits," which have been gouged from the working class, can obviously not be accepted in the case of public service strikes. What role indeed is played by the alleged "labor's disadvantage" justification for strikes when they occur in the public service? Unfortunately, the obvious need to abandon that argument has had no deterrent effect whatever. In many cases the exploitative power of collusion is enormous when employed in certain public service fields. State health or hospital employees, police, firemen, sanitation workers, school teachers and the like, for instance, have a fantastic ability to inflict harm on society if their demands are not met. And when such employees can threaten the health or safety of whole communities, if their claims for increased incomes are ignored, their powers of extortion are almost unbelievable.

What short-run gains *have* been attained by unionized workers, however, largely have been eaten away by inflation, which the strike-threat system has itself rendered expedient. Moreover, the strikers' gains have not been annexed mainly from the incomes of complementary parties— that is, the suppliers of assets. In addition, unproductive changes have been forced upon the composition of the community's aggregate assets stock. The technical form of this stock has consequently become adapted to suboptimal productive activities, and this in turn has reduced its general wage-multiplying power. The ultimate consequences, therefore, are distressingly

regressive, with the result that intended resistance to inequalities has in fact enormously aggravated inequalities. This last
point can be summarized as follows:

*In a society in which the strike-threat ex-
ists and is persistently pressed, investors
tend to avoid strike-prone industries, pro-
viding them with a lesser value of non-
versatile assets. The marginal prospective yields to investments in these
industries—effected by a falling supply
of capital—tend to equate with yields in
the industries which are not prone to the
threat. In other words, entrepreneurial
avoidance of prospective strike-threat
confiscation diverts the provision of specific assets to less productive and less
profitable forms. Yet, in every case, it is
in the interest of society in general and
the poor in particular that this diversion
shall cease. For it excludes investment
from activities bearing the highest yields
and hence, ceteris paribus, the highest
prospective demands for labor and maximum consumer satisfaction.*

It is the duty of managements to protect
their stockholders from exploitation, and
thereby protect society against the impoverishment created by man-made inequalities of income. The prime cause of such
inequalities has been, as we have tried to
show, capitulation to coercive strike-
threats or strike demands, or legal enact-

ment with similar consequences. Unfortunately, however, moral teaching has been grotesquely warped during the corruption of democratic ideals which has occurred during this century. Therefore, has it not been shown once again completely untenable that stockholders, through managements, take advantage of labor's inferior bargaining power, thereby exploiting workers? The only material possibilities of "exploitation" of the suppliers of labor are attributable, not to the suppliers of assets, but rather to (a) consumers, organized monopsonistically (a rare occurrence); or (b) the workers' own competitors, when one group of workers successfully bars others from entering activities of high productivity. Certainly, workers retaining employment can raise their own earning power by coercion; but that does not mean that they had been previously "robbed." Rather, in using coercive methods, they are "robbing" others. Therefore, they, *inter alia* and primarily, reduce the real earning power of the rest of society, on occasion inflict harm on comrades thrown into unemployment, and most undeniably, contribute to artificially high consumer prices borne by the whole community. Every restraint of competition in the labor market tends to have these effects.

All can be shown to gain from economic freedom. By exercising their right to "vote" under "consumers' sovereignty," the people exert their ultimate power to control the use made of society's productive activities and exemplify the egalitarian essence of our concept of social justice.

Moreover, under consumer's sovereignty, market-voting power is, as stressed previously, strongly weighted to favor the preferences of relatively poor and humble people. It is precisely against this exertion of egalitarian force that *every* coercive imposition of what we have called "nonmarket prices" is unquestionably aimed. We can think of no true exception. Unions, as well as most "liberal" or "labor" politicians, have been continuously resisting the achievement of relative working-class affluence, thereby perpetuating largely avoidable poverty.

The reasoning underlying this proposition, stressing merely consumers' detriment, is very simple. The argument, which could be easily refuted if it were wrong, is as follows. A rise in the price of shoes, whether due to a strike-threat or a rise in the price of leather, consequently will harm the poor purchaser more than it harms the rich purchaser.

In this perspective also, then, it is clear that the union's adversaries are not primarily the corporations whose stockholders the strikers believe (or pretend to believe) they are exploiting. It is those whom we call "the poor," whose incomes are gained in suboptimal occupations, on whom the costs of contrived scarcities imposed by privileged labor mainly fall, with unchallengeable regressiveness.

Society's tolerance of the private use of coercive power, under the delusion that it is a means of compensating for the "disadvantage of labor in bargaining," has been a blunder which every intelligent humanitarian must deplore, and against the continuance of which it is his most solemn duty to fight. It has made a mockery of justice in the relations of the individual to workers' organizations and the great society itself.

1. William Simon, *A Time for Truth* (New York: *Reader's Digest Press,* 1978), p. 166.
2. Peregrine Worsthorne, *The Socialist Myth,* 1971, p. 6.
3. Ibid, pp. 20-21.
4. Ibid, p. 7.
5. F.A. Hayek, *New Studies in Philosophy, Politics, Economics and the History of Ideas* (Chicago: U. Chicago Press, 1978), p. 57.
6. *Ibid.,* p. 57.
7. *Ibid.,* p. 58.
8. *Ibid.,* p. 63.
9. *Ibid.,* p. 60.
10. *Ibid.,* p. 62.
11. B.M. Anderson, *Economics and the*

Public Welfare, 1949, p. 387.

12. Hayek, *op. cit.,* p. 63.
13. *Ibid.*
14. *Ibid.,* p. 66.
15. *Ibid.,* p. 67.
16. An exception sometimes arises when a domestic or local producer must, for political reasons, openly be given preference. Even so, the argument for such discrimination is no stronger than the crudest argument for tariff protection, "price supports," or other sectionalist and impoverishing privileges of vote-acquisition origin.
17. The alternative opportunities will normally be lower remunerated opportunities but always, of course, less preferred opportunities.
18. Theoretically, it is essential to assume man-hours of unchanged average efficiency or productivity.
19. While this is true in each particular activity, the principle cannot be safely transferred to the whole economy without encountering the lurking danger of the fallacy of composition. (Quoted passage is from W.H. Hutt, *The Strike-Threat System,* Arlington House, 1973, pp. 220-221.)
20. There is, as we have seen, an entrepreneurial aspect about nearly all economic actions. Indeed there always is when remuneration is based on "pay-

ment by the piece" or other forms of "payment by results." There is, for instance, an entrepreneurial aspect about choosing an occupation, as well as in spending time and income in acquiring particular skills (investing in "human capital"). Hence, some elements of "profit" are scattered through labor's remuneration as a whole.

21. In most contemporary discussions of "social justice", the term's connotation equates it with "equality of condition" as distinct from "equality of opportunity." But the latter is among the conditions which are normally necessary for the achievement of the optimal measure of the former. Hence our phrase, "the principle of social justice", reflects the philosophy of a system in which the greatest possible degree of long-term equality of income is sought, by methods which are compatible with maximum freedom of contract and freedom of choice.

22. Although Wicksteed once argued (with tongue in cheek) that in a competitive society, that is, under pure *laissez-faire*, a butcher would be remunerated higher than a surgeon. The odium attaching to the butcher's trade, he suggested, and the honor and responsibility attaching to the work of

the surgeon would raise the remuneration of the former and reduce that of the latter.

23. Strike-threat consequences have not been the only form in which the lower income groups have had their potentialities of material progress attentuated. For instance, welfarism is believed by many to have been an important factor in the demoralization of the less opulent classes. Poor schooling, also due, according to many concerned Americans, to schools being run for the benefit of the teachers rather than for the improvement of the powers of the pupils, is blamed by some. And those kinds of vote-buying which take the form of price supports in agriculture, tariff protection in industry, licensing for occupations with the real objective of protecting the incomes of lobbying groups (like opticians, plumbers, hairdressers, pharmacists, nurses and physicians) are the source of another kind of impoverishment.

ECONOMISTS AND THE PUBLIC REVISITED

by
Arthur Shenfield

In 1936 Professor Hutt published his *Economists and the Public*. It was his first major work. In 1930 he had published his little gem, *The Theory of Collective Bargaining*, which has remained a classic piece of work and is the foundation of his later work on labour problems, for example, *The Strike Threat System*. However, *The Theory* was of narrow compass and compressed length. In *Economists and the Public* he embarked on an excursion over a very broad field, ranging over many fundamental social and political, as well as economic, problems.

1936 was not a propitious year for an economist of Hutt's views to achieve acclaim or success in persuasion. It was the year of Keynes' *General Theory*. Against the powerful wind and tide raised by that work, Hutt had little chance of carrying with him more than a few among the broad intellectual public to whom he addressed his work. As it happens, although his manuscript was already in page proofs when the *General Theory* appeared, he and his publishers managed to insert a succinct and perceptive note on it in the body of Hutt's book, an excellent feat of publishing skill unlikely to be attempted, not to mention achieved, by publishers of our day. Readers of Hutt's two later full-length works on Keynes will not be surprised to learn that on the very morrow of the *General Theory's* appearance, he was able to draw attention to some of its ultimately disastrous consequences.

However, the Keynesian putsch was not the main reason why, in 1936, Hutt was likely to be little more than a voice crying in the wilderness. On the issues which he addressed, orthodox economists other than the Austrians (who at the time numbered Robbins among them), had become flabby long before the onset of the Keynesian revolution. As a result, academic economics, at least in Britain and outside the London School of Economics, presented only a weak and qualified defense to the intellectual assault on the free market system. Mainstream economists still believe the market system to be the best available, on balance, but they spent much of their time and effort in exposing its supposed defects and limitations. Scholarly integrity appeared to require that cases of alleged market failure should be punctiliously brought into view by supporters of the market system themselves. Hence, the numerous intellectuals of various kinds who mounted a constant assault on the market system—and looking back on them over the past half-century one finds many of their criticisms and assertions to have been of a staggering naiveté—could easily brush aside so doubtful a defense when they appealed to the public.

Hutt's position was very different. He admitted, indeed emphasized, that the market system's operation was defective. But in his view that was in no way a reflection of any defect in the market system itself. It was the result of institutional and other impediments to the system which enabled anti-social sectional interests to seize and maintain a power to thwart the general interest which the market system, if unshackled, would splendidly serve. Hence his defense of the system rested upon a forthright attack upon the influences which first shackled the market and then blamed the market for the defects which they themselves had produced.

Not that Hutt necessarily got the matter quite right. His attack was splendid. But then, in my opinion, he weakened his position by embracing certain errors, as I conceive them to be, one of which, I know from many cordial but contentious conversations with him, he has cleaved to throughout his life. I shall discuss below what I believe these errors to be.

The purpose of "Economists and the

Public" was not merely to present a piece of economic analysis, even if extended to an examination of its related social and political problems. As its title implied, it was intended to probe the public mind and to discover why it had slid away from the influence of well-established and authentic economic doctrine. What, he asked, had caused reputable economists to lose the grip which they had once had on the public mind? Why was it that, as Bagehot said, "No real Englishman in his secret soul was ever sorry for the death of an economist"?[1] Were there perhaps weaknesses or errors in economic doctrine itself to which the loss of influence could be attributed? How could the influence of economists be restored? These questions led Hutt into very broad fields of enquiry.

He began with an examination of what, borrowing terms from Robert Briffault,[2] he called custom-thought, power-thought, and rational-thought. Custom-thought was a powerful impediment to the operation of the market system, because it resisted and clogged the element of change and adaptability which was an essential part of it. It was a constant readiness to adopt, welcome, and profit by change that enabled the market system to operate successfully.

Power-thought was an even stronger impediment than custom-thought. Custom-thought could not easily masquerade as new, a weakness in our society where many people are captivated by whatever presents itself as new. Power-thought, though old, maleficent, destructive, and unjust, could masquerade as new, beneficent, constructive, and just. Both custom-thought and power-thought protected established positions and sectional interests which were inimical to the general interest. In particular, they thwarted the beneficent operation of competition, for it was by way of competition that established positions were dissolved and sectional interests eroded. Power-thought was the more baleful of the two because it added the great strength of selfishness, especially that of group selfishness, to the ideas which it propounded. It imbued the selfishness of groups with strong feelings of community, comradeship and fellow-feeling. Custom-thought and power-thought together set up a most powerful obstacle to rational-thought. The great virtue of the classical economists lay in their detachment from sectional interest as well as in their mastery of rational thought. One of the most offensive calumnies on them was the allegation that they stood for the sectional interests of the capitalist class.

The essence of the matter lay in the understanding of the nature and effect of competition. Competition was the shield and support of the general interest. Being the great benefactor of the poor and the weak in society, it was essentially an egalitarian force, which was one reason why it was hated. For the socially just type of egalitarianism is highly irksome to entrenched interests of many kinds, notably those of organized labour. At the same time the self-styled egalitarians of socialist parties and propagandists hated competition because, not understanding it, they thought that it favored the strong against the weak, the successful against the unsuccessful. They failed to see that its favors were not for the entrenched strong against the hapless weak, but for success against failure in the service of others, especially in the service of the masses. Hutt's treatment of these matters was admirably accurate, especially in his refutation of popular pseudo-history about the supposed degradation of the workers in early industrialism and in his exposition of the true nature of the much maligned laissez-faire. Of course it was laissez-faire which brought freedom and opportunity to the masses for the first time in the history of mankind.

He then proceeded to argue that classical economics became flabby after the 1860's, as I have noted above. Here he singled out John Stuart Mill for particular criticism. According to Hutt, Mill began to find excuses for influences and policies inimical to the beneficent laissez-faire system. In particular Mill set the fashion among economists for praising trade unions with faint damns, leading to respect for, and even benevolence towards, them (while of course deploring the more ugly manifestations of union power). Thus resistance to the claims of sectional interests became progressively weaker, except in the case of international trade.[3] Later elements of historicism and other features of scientism entered into respectable economic thinking (though fortunately not as much in Britain as in Germany or the United States), and still further muddied the waters of classical economics.

In a largely hostile review of *Economists and the Public,* Jacob Viner castigated Hutt magisterially for attributing Mill's alleged errors to "political ambitions and the craving for popular approval."[4] Though Hutt had said something on similar lines, it was in much more restrained terms. Mill did not have significant political ambitions even though elected to Parliament, but he did give some obeisance to politics.[5] He did not crave for popular approval, but he did seek to accommodate himself to the new-found popular approbation given to the New Model unions.[6] In my opinion, Hutt was right and Viner wrong on this issue.

In seeking ways to re-establish the legitimate intellectual influence of economists, Hutt first analyzed the nature of authority in opinion. In the natural sciences the conditions which establish authority, and thus general acceptance, are not very difficult to determine, which does not mean that authoritative scientific doctrines are necessarily true or beyond refutation. On the contrary, the history of the natural sciences is a history of the refutation of doctrines once accepted as authoritative. Nevertheless, the role of authority in science is legitimate and essential. It gives scientists a set of bearings as they embark on their explorations. It would be extremely counterproductive for scientists to assume that nothing is already agreed and that therefore everything must be established *de novo*. Even though we know that eminent scientists may prove to be wrong and that someone labelled a crank or a crackpot may turn out to be right, the distinction between a reputable scientist and a crank is very important. It would be enormously wasteful of time and effort if the theories of cranks had to be tested with the same respectful attention as those of reputable scientists. Hutt's account of the conditions which justify authority in opinion was apt and illuminating.

However, authority in economics is far more difficult to establish than in the natural sciences, even though economics is the best developed of all the social sciences, and though there are some basic propositions which are accepted by all reputable persons who bear the title of economist. Hutt was thinking of such a degree of authority among professional economists, notoriously among the most disputatious of men, as would cause their doctrines to be accepted as scientific truth by the general public! If a layman is asked to accept some basic doctrine of physics or chemistry, he has little difficulty in doing so because his interests and emotions are unlikely to be affected. But even the simplest and clearest doctrine in economics, such as, for example, the proposition that fixing a price below the market clearing level will, *ceteris paribus,* produce a shortage of supply, may strike a sensitive nerve in the layman and cause him to reject it out of hand; this takes no account of the fact that there are numerous politicians whose careers are based upon finding and exciting such sensitive nerves in the general public. It is true that for somewhat more than half a century, say from Adam Smith to Nassau Senior, economists did establish something like a respected authority among the general public, but the social and political conditions which favored such a circumstance were very special. At that time intellectual society in Britain was small and hence could be of an elevated character. It was possible for public opinion to be shaped and led by men of intellectual seriousness and moral integrity. It was a time of the confluence of the best elements in the aristocratic and bourgeois virtues. In economics it was not only the men who became world famous, such as Ricardo, Malthus, McCulloch and Senior, who displayed these qualities, but also the men of lesser fame, such as Torrens, Tooke, Fullarton, and several others. With the social and political democratization of Britain, such circumstances did not last, and with the benefit of hindsight we can see that they could not last.[7]

Hutt made a brave try at delineating the conditions to be observed by economists in order to establish their authority. They must be ivory tower men par excellence (incidentally the very characteristic which induces politicians and men of affairs to scoff at them). They must not be active politicians (before World War II the London School of Economics permitted its faculty members to be Members of Parliament if they could get elected, a license which Hutt vigorously objected to). They must not be attached to or employed by any sectional group with an economic interest. They must not be active in business. They must so order their personal investments as to be free from temptation to favour a sectional interest (cf. the blind trusts of modern Government Ministers and high officials). The prescription was admirable but hardly practicable, though of course Hutt himself could have passed these stern tests with flying colors. He was probably one of the few distinguished economists who could.[8] Always a man of honor, it was not in his character to lay down tests for others which he could not pass himself.

I come now to what I believe to be Hutt's errors. This is no place for a disputatious argument of the kind which we witness often in the academic world. I do indeed come in this essay to praise Hutt, not to bury any part of his outstanding contribution to our understanding of economic affairs. But as we all know, the very greatest economists and philosophers of the past have all been found to have mixed grains of error with their monumental discoveries of truth; and it would be surprising if even the most distinguished of our contemporaries differed in this regard from their predecessors.

Consider first Hutt's doctrine of consumer's sovereignty. This looms large in "Economists and the Public," as it does in his other works. Let us note at once that if consumers' sovereignty meant only that in the free market system the consumer has an unqualified right to buy or not to buy what the producer offers him and therefore to send the producer packing without compensation if the offer is unacceptable, it would be unexceptionable. However it goes further. It seems to attribute to the consumer a right to freedom of choice and action superior to that of the producer. This does not follow from the unqualified right of the consumer to buy or not to buy what the producer offers. It therefore needs separate and additional argument, which I have regretfully to say here cannot in my opinion be successfully sustained.[9]

Of course in practice Hutt is generally in accord with all other champions of the free economy in defense of the rights of consumers. For the sectional interests which pervert the economy and shackle the market, calling in aid the unjustifiable protection and support of the state, are almost always producer interests. In the defense of the legitimate rights of the consumer against such producer interests, there is no more doughty battler than Hutt.

In *Economists and the Public* he poured scorn on Chief Justice White's concept of the Rule of Reason, as stated in the Standard Oil Case. In this Hutt was right, for White's enunciation of the concept was sadly muddled, and largely useless to lawyers and economists. But the thrust of Hutt's criticism was in favor of an absolutely unqualified *per se* rule against all agreements limiting output, a rule which both analysis and experience have shown to be inimical not only to economic improvement but also to competition itself. Of course, like other non-Austrian free market economists, he had not grasped the fundamental truth that free competition is a force which drives enterprise both away from and towards equilibrium. In this he bemused himself by fastening on to a presumed fundamental difference between contrived and natural scarcity. On examination, the difference proves to be less clear and fundamental than he thought.[10]

The second major error which in my opinion Hutt fell into in *Economists and the Public* was graver than the concept of consumers' sovereignty. But there is this difference. Consumers' sovereignty has remained a Huttian doctrine to this day, whereas my impression is that this other error, as I believe it to be, was abandoned by him a good many years ago. He was led to endorse state action to redistribute incomes and wealth and to abridge freedom of bequest in *Economists and the Public* by the following reasoning:

1. Competition, the flywheel or mainspring of the beneficent free market economy, was in essence an egalitarian force.

2. The main egalitarian thrust of competition was towards equality of opportunity. It was through equality of opportunity that the elevation of the masses could happen.

3. Since the development and maintenance of the legal framework of the competitive economy was a proper and necessary function of the State in the system of laissez-faire (contrary to the misunderstandings of laissez-faire by its enemies), it followed that the State should use its power to remove impediments to equality of opportunity.

4. Inequality of wealth was a major im-

pediment to equality of opportunity. Therefore the State should redistribute wealth to an extent and in a manner reasonably necessary to produce a practicable measure of equality of opportunity.

5. Since freedom of bequest or inheritance of large estates was a powerful impediment to equality of opportunity, a major element in State action should be the limitation of freedom of inheritance (in this matter Hutt was an admiring supporter, not a critic, of Mill, who had expressed the same opinion).

Thus Hutt was led to endorse the Rignano Plan,[11] redistribution of incomes by "progressive" taxation (though recognizing the dangers of such taxation if unwisely applied), and unconditional State subsidies for education, which he believed to be essential though he preferred State loans in principle. He found the family to be a potent source of inequality of opportunity or, as he put it, "a bulwark against economic equality," though he shrank from endorsing positive State action against the family. He even went so far as to endorse restriction of freedom of emigration of those who had been provided with education or training at State expense, once this had produced equality of opportunity.

The free world's experience in recent years has shown us how slippery and dangerous a concept equality of opportunity can be, if it is not properly understood, and with hindsight we can see how Hutt was misled by it. The only true principle of equality of opportunity is *"le carriére ouverte aux talents."* Unfortunately in our time it has become twisted into something entirely different, namely that life's races should be fixed so that all start from the same position or are compensated if they do not. Thus we have the abomination of affirmative action, so-called equal pay for equal work (meaning equal pay for unequal work), the Equal Rights Amendment (meaning the Unequal Rights Amendment), and other propositions and devices now familiar.

Despite the blemishes of these errors, *Economists and the Public* was a great book. It never received the recognition from the scholarly world which it deserved. The world of 1936 was bemused by Keynes and numerous others. How much pain and failure it might have spared itself if it had given heed to the main thesis of *Economists and the Public*. Though it appeared nearly 50 years ago and does seem dated in more than a few respects, its main thesis is as fresh and up-to-date as ever: The source of the major evils which beset our half-free society and economy is the assault by sectional interests upon the general interest. This, after all, is the essential nature of the malady which afflicts our present bemused and perverted democracy. What is presented to us by our politicians and our less intelligent intellectuals is nothing more than the cobbled together programs of a coalition of sectional interests. Hutt's problem of 1936 is still our problem in 1986; indeed, it may be more menacing in 1986 than in 1936 because his warnings were not heeded.

1. Quoted by Hutt on page 131 of his *Economists and the Public* (London: J. Cape, 1936).
2. Robert Briffault, *The Making of Humanity* (London: G. Allen and Unwin, 1919).
3. As late as 1929 the British Labour Party, *mirabile dictu* and with a fantastic failure to grasp the logic of its own policies, still claimed to be a Free Trade party. The Liberal Party, the traditional party of Free Trade, had also by 1929 taken on board an array of programs and policies inconsistent with Free Trade, but it too failed to see the inconsistency.
4. *Journal of Political Economy.* Vol. 46, August 1938, p. 575.
5. His famous speech to the Westminster electors shows how free he was from the common kind of political ambition.
6. The New Model unions arose in the 1850's for the organization of certain

skilled workers. These were, "business unions" of the kind later developed by Sam Gompers in the USA.

7. An illuminating example of similar elevation in public discussion was presented by the Federalist Papers, written by Hamilton, Madison and Jay for the newspaper reading public of New York. Can one imagine that essays of such quality could be put day after day or week after week to the newspaper readers of present-day New York, or any other city in the world? Even the *Neue Zürcher Zeitung*, no doubt the most serious paper in the world, could hardly dare to do so.

8. It may be noted that Ricardo, who was Hutt's *beau idéal* of an economist, had been a stockbroker and was a Member of Parliament during much of his most fertile period as an economist. However, the conditions of his time were such that it was possible for him to have the perfect qualities of integrity and detachment which Hutt's tests were intended to produce, despite his business and political career.

9. The argument for consumers' sovereignty is of course to be found at length in Hutt's works. For what I believe to be a very persuasive argument against it, see Murray Rothbard, *Man, Economy and State* (Princeton, NJ:

Van Nostrand, 1962), Vol. 2, pp. 561-573. The debate is an excellent example of the divergence between The British classical tradition, in which Hutt is steeped, and the insights of the "Austrians."

10. See *inter alia*, Dominick T. Armentano, *The Myths of Antitrust* (New Rochelle, New York: Arlington House, 1972); Robert H. Bork, *The Antitrust Paradox* (New York: Basic Books, 1978); Yale Brozen, *Concentration Mergers, and Public Policy* (New York: Macmillan, 1982); and Arthur Shenfield, *Myth and Reality of Antitrust* (London: Institute of Economic Affairs, 1983).

11. Nowadays little is heard of the Rignano Plan, but in the 1920's and 1930's it made a considerable stir. It was a plan for a system of taxation under which an individual's own accumulations of property during his lifetime were free from heavy death duties, while that part of his property which represented inheritance or gifts from others was very heavily taxed on his death, the incidence varying according to the relative age of various portions of what the deceased had inherited or received as gifts, and according to the relationship to him of the beneficiaries of his bequests.

COLLECTIVE BARGAINING
or ECONOMIC PLURALISM

by
Ralph Horwitz

*Only rarely is any attitude formulated
with the profound and majestic momen-
tum of a magnum opus. Still more rarely
does the appearance of a book on social
thought cause us to take stock of our intellectual heritage. Professor Hutt has
succeeded in this handsome volume in
representing the attitude of liberal economic orthodoxy in what can only be described as the grand manner. There can
be no doubt that this book will remain on
our shelves among the handful of others
in which our traditions of sociological
thinking are gravely inscribed.*

—The *New Statesman* review of *Economists and the Public* by W.H. Hutt
(1936)

Contrary to the comment above by the
New Statesman, Bill Hutt—mentor, friend
of half a century, and now in his eighty-
seventh year as *enfant terrible* of latterday
economics—published his *magnum opus*
six years earlier in the form of an essay.

His *Theory of Collective Bargaining* was a short, scholarly and highly theoretical exercise. In his preface, Professor Hutt wrote: "The essay is brief but brevity I claim as a virtue. It is absolutely untopical . . . it is strange that there should be a complete absence of any modern treatise on the theory of trade unions, for there is a colossal literature on its organization and history."

From the vantage point of the 1980s, more than 50 years later, his "history, analysis and criticism of the principal theories which have sought to explain the effects of trade unions and employers' associations upon the distribution of the product of industry" has a topicality and vitality of critical import. Indeed, on the assumptions that (a) there is political economy but not economic science and (b) money supply control is a necessary but not sufficient condition for eliminating inflation, then trade unionism and its concomitant collective bargaining is the single most crucial—and crucifying—issue of the political economy of western capitalism as of the 1980s.

Hutt's *Theory of Collective Bargaining*, from such a standpoint, continues to be more than the "brilliant essay," as Ludwig von Mises described it in his preface to the New American edition of 1954. It is, rather, as Mises went on to say, a critical analysis of the arguments advanced by economists from Adam Smith on down and by the spokesmen of the unions in favor of the thesis that unionism can raise wages above the market level without harm to anybody other than the 'exploiters'. As such, the *Theory of Collective Bargaining* is of the utmost use not only to every student of economics but to everybody else who wants to form a well-founded opinion about one of the most vital and most controversial issues of our age.

The collectivism of British trade unionism is at an apogee of controversy and importance in relation to the immediate future of the world's original industrial nation. Surely no institution is more fateful for the destiny of the British political economy than its trade unionism. Yet the theory of trade unionism as collective bargaining continues almost unexamined in the tumult of debate, both academic and public, over industrial relations. If ever *Hamlet* has been played without *The Prince,* then the non-stop theatre of industrial relations is staged daily and performed without any meaningful theory of collective bargaining.

Is there an indeterminacy about the wage of labour as the market price for work, or is labour a product like any other product? Does the assertion that the worker has 'only his or her labour to sell' place the worker at a disadvantage in the competitive market in which labour is bought and sold? Can the employer exploit a superior bargaining power—does he indeed have it? Such questioning, of course, challenges articles of faith. Postulating that labour is a product subject to the pricing forces of the marketplace is not just emotive but explosive to many ears. Hutt's essay is an analysis based on such questioning and postulation. It begins with the delineation of the fixed wages-fund and fixed work-fund propositions, and their refutation by both unfamiliar and famous economists.

It would probably surprise contemporary trade unionists that Adam Smith provides the authority for some of unionism's most cherished dogmas about collective bargaining. The author of *The Wealth of Nations* is not the Left's favourite economist but his views on what was to become known as the theory of collective bargaining arose from the subsistence theory of the human condition. "Upon all ordinary occasions," he wrote, "the masters have the advantage in the dispute and [can force] the men into a compliance with their terms." It was Adam Smith too, writes Hutt, who was the first to talk about "the funds destined for the payment of labour" and thereby Smith was led to views about the workers' disadvantage similar to some of the significant names in classical economics, including J.R. McCulloch, John Stuart Mill, and Alfred Marshall.

Smith's explanation of "this vague power," as Hutt describes it, the masters' [employers'] advantage in the pricing of labour, contained three separate ideas. First, there were particular combinations of masters who agreed to force down wages to subsistence level. Second, there was "a tacit but uniform combination" among employers to keep wages down. Third, although in the long run the workman might be "as necessary to his master as his master is to him, [the necessity] is not so immediate." Smith claimed that masters, "though they did not employ a single workman, could generally live a year or two upon the stocks which they have already acquired," while workmen "could not subsist a week, few could subsist a month, and scarce any a year without employment." Smith concluded that these factors accounted for the employers' power to force wages down to the subsistence level.

Hutt forthwith declares Smith's theorizing to be "empty" and that Smith gave no explanation for what the author of *The Wealth of Nations* simply presumed was self-evident. Smith thought the limits of employers' power to be determined not by the individual employee's minimum survival needs, but by the minimal survival requirements of his family as the generative source of labour supply into the future. Hutt notes that Smith observed wages often ruled at levels considerably higher than subsistence level, so he limited his theory to "ordinary occasions," while also qualifying the minimum subsistence wages paid to be the lowest "consistent with common humanity."

Hutt recognizes the significance of historical evidence for such a theory of wages, particularly for the allegation that masters habitually formed themselves into combinations to force wages down. He also notes that workmen's combinations were present in Smith's time no less, and perhaps no more, than masters' combinations. On the record, Hutt finds that "throughout the greater part of the nineteenth century the extent of combination of capitalism for the express purpose of settling wages was negligible." In this kind of sociological inquiry, perhaps we ought to concede that there is no non-ideological answer to: who started forming combinations in labour markets, employers or employees? Perhaps positive science can conclude no more than which came first, the chicken or the egg? It is the great merit of Hutt's theorizing to ask the more relevant question about the determinants of competitive wage-price and then to analyze how wage bargains may be determined in cases where competition has been eliminated by the two-sided, or bilateral, monopoly of trade unionism and employers' association.

Tacit or unorganized understandings among employers to sustain customary wages must be regarded as the stuff of both fact and fiction. In traditional societies and in backward sectors of advancing societies, employers may strongly or stubbornly resist market factors favouring higher wages for work supplied. As Professor Hutt wryly notes, Pepys complains that having paid his first maid three pounds a year and supplying her with clothes, "a fat Welsh girl who has just come out of the country, scarce understood a word of English, capable of nothing but washing, scouring and sweeping the rooms . . . (receives) six guineas a year, besides a guinea for tea." Pepys was not expressing a unique complaint. Doubtless, however, if the daily observations of the fat Welsh girl were available to us, they would reflect a contrary sense of use and abuse.

Contemporary academic pontification about industrial relations, exhaustive though it is, does not yet approach the quantum of opinion expressed through the centuries about the duties and rights of employer and employee in domestic service. In the 1980s the subject only seems of literary interest, since there are virtually no domestic servants left in any advanced capitalist society—indeed, *because* it is both capitalist and advanced. The current compulsion on all of us, economists and non-economists alike, to do our own vacuuming, stack our own dishes in the washing machine, and heat up our own precooked cans, sharpens the consciousness, if not the analysis, of advantage-disadvantage with respect to domestic labour.

The example of domestic service employment is not offered by Hutt himself, but it serves well to illustrate his theorizing on the critical issues of market determinacy and of the wage as the demand-supply price of labour. And the example does so for a form of employment, menial and demeaning by general acknowledgment and in which exploitation of the uneducated, unskilled worker is regarded as self-evident. If, on examination, there is neither theoretical nor empirical support for exploitation by masters of servants in the household then, *pro tanto,* all the lore about capitalistic exploitation of industrial workers pertains properly to that received wisdom which substitutes sophistry for sophistication. The theory and evidence on domestic service readily exposes how misinformed Marxist and neo-Marxist argument on capital-labour exploitation has been and is. The very disappearance of domestic servants and their reincarnation as hotel-catering workers, shop and office labour similarly exposes how little Karl Marx really recognized the dynamics of economic history.

In the Leftist credo, ignorance and lack of reserves in the independent individual worker so facilitate exploitation that only collective bargaining prevents the grossest abuse by the capitalist employer of the ignorance of the individually weak. No trade union of domestic servants has organized itself effectively for collective bargaining. Does that mean the market for domestic labour is imperfect, in the sense that there is such absence of competitive determinants as to establish ignorance of market wage rates for domestics among both 'masters' and 'servants'—and thus an indeterminant range of lower and higher wage for uniform (or largely identical) work? Only if there is such an indeterminant wage-range would the possibility of exploitation come into being.

Fiction is not necessarily empirical truth but, nonetheless, the literature of almost all societies has its grumblings of employers having to concede 'outrageous' demands—or do their own thing. This may prove no more than that 'masters' dislike paying-up. It strongly supports the proposition, however, that communication/ information about market realities is exceptionally effective in domestic employment. There clearly is a grapevine of communication among the most uneducated, even illiterate, of the servant class that serves to carry the most up-to-the-minute data on ruling wages and service conditions with the immediacy of any video screen linked to a computerized store of on-line information. Indeed, there can be few areas of employment in which appreciation of 'worth' is more continuously evaluated and re-evaluated by both sides than in the master-servant intimacy of domestic work.

Neither master nor domestic ever stops making comparisons. By its very nature, such appreciation is entirely subjective, yet such an unceasing process of evaluation and re-evaluation yields the objective market price or wage for domestic service with a sensitivity to intelligence and expectations comparable to the market for equity shares.

The marginal productivity theory of wage determination is empirically substantiated in domestic service to a degree matched only perhaps by piece-rate bricklayers on building sites, or so-called temporaries in office jobs or straight commission salesmen in insurance. Wage-bargaining in all such non-unionized employment precludes exploitation by either side because the market process of competition ensures, firstly, continuous disclosure of innumerable individual bargains as information and, secondly, a continuing matching of marginal productivity for each specific job performed with knowledge of the market price or ruling wage for that service.

Ruling *earnings* may of course be low as compared to earnings in other jobs or may even be used to construct a 'poverty datum line'. This does not, however, invalidate that *wages* are determinate. In domestic service—the classic case of non-unionized individual bargaining—there is no empirical substance for an indeterminacy theory rising from a lack of bargaining power by way of ignorance or lack of reserves by the individual low-earning servant.

The significance of Hutt's general disproof of 'indeterminacy' is readily misunderstood—and misrepresented. His argument does not claim that a prevailing or ruling wage for servants or shopgirls or hotel workers or typists at any point in time gives such persons low or high earnings. The argument is that wages as a market-determined price for labour is no more and no less determined by the market process than the market price determined for peas and corn. Whether two individual servants are or are not alike as two peas in a pod is as much subjective as objective. Perhaps every master regards servants as 'all the same' or, indifferently, as 'hands'. The subjectivity-objectivity is matched and related by the market process so as to determine the wage rate equated to marginal productivity. There is no range of indeterminacy within which 'exploitation' can operate.

The process of information-evaluation-communication that is the market process will continuously operate to spread information about the evaluation of marginal productivity as assessed by servants, thereby constituting the supply of domestics and, as assessed by employers, to constitute the demand for domestics. The market process will *ipso facto* establish and communicate data of wage as marginal productivity; the information-evaluation will yield a determinate wage or price for the product of domestic labour.

The fact that there are variations in wages paid to individual servants as individuals by individual employers does not establish "indeterminateness." It merely establishes that individuals may be as closely alike as two peas in a pod, in which case there is a ruling wage for all cooks; or it establishes that a chef is as different from a cook as *petit pois* is unlike any other pea-pod—and priced accordingly for its 'difference' or uniqueness.

Vin ordinaire and Chateau Lafite both begin in a vineyard. The price of the former is determined by suppliers of ordinary wine to drinkers who are non-discriminate, for whatever reasons, in fermented grapes. The price of Chateau Lafite is established by the bargaining between the sole supplier of an extraordinary vintage; discriminating palates may require an auction market to remove the element of indeterminateness from the monopoly supply-side. When the element of monopoly is bilateral—that is, when those who sell collectivize their supply and those who buy collectivize their demand—true indeterminateness emerges. Indeterminateness is the consequence of collective bargaining on both sides of the bargain.

Where a trade union as a monopoly supplier of closed-shop labour confronts an employer's organization as a monopoly buyer of such closed-shop labour, such indeterminateness is a range for the exploitation of power, with the balance of power shifting in favour of trade unionism as the capital structure and technology of the economy grows more sophisticated. Pull out a computer plug in the banking system of capitalism to confirm that this is the reality—and not Marxist myth. Whether such growing trade union power has redistributed the 'product' of the economy in favour of 'workers' against 'capitalists' is not readily answered by theory, history, or statistics. Since 1930, when Hutt first published his *Theory of Collective Bargaining,* the half century of extraordinary economic development has been a chain of causes and consequences in which consequences become causes. Generalizations cannot be incontestably sustained against an alternative set of hypotheses or empirical propositions. The role of the state and trade unionism in promoting or frustrating living standards is particularly an interpretation of statistical allegiance. The right to work is no less a presentation or misrepresentation of a basic human right. 'Right to Work' is a street-march banner-claim against governments' failure to offer jobs on terms acceptable to the unemployed; or the 'Right to Work' is a Texas law (and a few like-minded legislatures of the United States) represented as the legal entitlement of an individual to offer himself-herself for employment on terms voluntarily preferred by that individual without constraint by trade unionism or state regulation.

In their time, millions of people have worked at what they saw as the menial chores of domestic service. When preferred jobs presented new opportunities, those millions abandoned housework—neither trade unionism nor state regulation being involved in the process of the right to work first in and then out of domestic services. Many moved to the related hotel-catering jobs, where unionism and governmental regulation has fitfully tried to impose minimum wage-working conditions. To whose benefit? Hutt's theorizing has always insisted that such intervention in the market process delays the poor escaping their poverty. Good faith and bad faith combine in delusion and propaganda to deny and frustrate self-advancement to those compelled to queue at the bottom of life's ladder.

In our economies of advancing technology, the job characteristics of the highly competitive hotel-catering trade are perhaps unique in presenting both a ladder and an escalator—always provided there is no forcible exclusion from the queue by minimum wage-working conditions imposed by the state, trade unions, or "public conscience." As a business, hotel catering is highly diverse, highly competitive, and highly entrepreneurial. As such, only misguided regulation diminishes opportunity to get in at the bottom and climb some way to the top. Where competition among employers is unrestricted, there is a nigh-impossibility of "exploitation." The lowliest, dirtiest job in the most disagreeable establishment is an escape from even more dire poverty—above all for the immigrant emigrating from nil or negative productivity in a Malthusian trap. Not only does unregulated competition in hotel-catering offer an escape, but for many it has been an escape route. There are men and their sons still alive at the very top of heavy capitalized, world-wide hotel-catering empires who gained their backgrounds at a boarding house or a milkbar. Read the business history of Conrad Hilton or Lord Charles Forte for stories of thousands of the modestly successful.

Forty-three years after his 1930 essay Hutt returned to the analysis of the economic consequences of collective bargaining in his *The Strike-Threat System* (Arlington House, 1973). He again took up the crucial issue of "exploitation." With its *"Workers of the world, unite: you have nothing to lose but your chains,"* the *Communist Manifesto* culminated Marx's sociology of capitalism exploitation. Hutt's conceptualization was rather less evocative and rather more rigorous.

I define 'exploitation' as any action taken whether or not through discernable private coercion (collusion) or governmental

> *coercion, which reduces the value of the*
> *property or income of another person, or*
> *prevents that value from rising as rap-*
> *idly as it otherwise would, unless this ef-*
> *fect is brought about through: (a)*
> *dissolving some privilege, or (b) substi-*
> *tuting some cheaper method (labor-*
> *saving or capital saving) of achieving any*
> *objective; or (c) expressing a change in*
> *consumer's preferences, or (d) democrati-*
> *cally authorized taxation.*

The *Strike-Threat System* concerns itself
entirely with the exploitation of workers
by investors or investors by workers (investors being synonymous with entrepreneurs
in Hutt's usage). Hutt's substitution of 'investors' for 'capital' is consequential. It
carries with it the implication that investment, in totality, cannot be locked-in, permanently, by a labour strike so that
"forcing up the price of labor in different
firms, occupations or industries does not
affect an income redistribution *from inves-*
tors in general to workers in general." For
Hutt, investment decisions are entrepreneurial decisions and "these decisions,
which are being continuously made, are in
every case concerned with retaining, replacing, accumulating or decumulating the
physical resources employed in various
possible combinations of, in certain specific activities, together with the retaining,
recruiting or displacing of labour in accordance with this process." The use of capital

equipment, materials, and labor in any activity, he continues, will not occur unless some entrepreneurial remuneration is deemed possible for every increment of resources invested in that activity. And, he concludes, (thus) a firm will not retain, replace or accumulate additional assets unless the prospective output values of each *increment* exceed the corresponding current and prospective input values by more than the rate of interest.

The conceptual logic comes down to the argument that entrepreneurial choice can anticipate and allow for the strike threat or collective power to fix wage rates. If an entrepreneur avoids commitment of capital, then there is no possibility of exploitation. Choice is thus not constrained. But what of decision? What of commitment in specific productive equipment or asset structure? Hutt would answer that what has happened is an entrepreneurial forecasting error. "Hence in general," he writes, "there can be no 'exploitation' of retained, replaced or accumulated capital, except on the assumption of entrepreneurial forecasting errors."

Hutt is not oblivious, of course, to the target set up by a specific commitment of specific capital as an investment. He puts it as follows:

Having stated this broad thesis (of non-exploitability), it is essential to stress what it does not imply; labor costs im-

> *posed by duress immediately do change the property rights of individuals or groups. The strike threat works much like a gun threat. In theory it can, therefore, redistribute property as a street robber can, to the extent to which people carry thievable assets. I am not questioning anything as obvious as that. Investors who have not foreseen the use of the strike weapon resemble the traveler who carries with him large sums of money.*

Those who have known Bill Hutt for a lifetime will recognize the penchant for the shockable analogy—and be moved to amusement and not to ire. This obviously excludes the trade unionists or the solemn Left, but even a conservative capitalist (and a friendly academic) may hesitate to embrace such representation of ascribed naivete. The microeconomic nature of investment—and all investment decisions are fundamentally microeconomic in being made as an individual, not totality of, commitment and decision—is such that, first, specific commitment to a specific structure of capital as non-money or 'production-function' is ineluctable. Second, the retaining and replacing of that structure of capital as a production capability is a time structure of continuing investment choice-decision in which the timing of the related short run and long run replacements is readily open to exploitation by the trade union.

Perhaps the fundamental difficulty with Hutt's "forecasting error" by the entrepreneurial investor is its conceptual legitimacy. Surely an entrepreneurial investor commits his venturesomeness to the future. That is, he commits himself to uncertainty, since futurity and uncertainty are one and the same thing. Such commitment is not 'risk' in the since that Frank Knight distinguished the insurable risk against uninsurable uncertainty. There is no way the entrepreneurial investor can insure against a quantifiable risk-occurrence of strikes, though in the late 1970s in Britain the incidence of strikes had reached a regularity that led the Confederation of British Industry, an employers' organization, to try to introduce strike-risk insurance. There has been much academic work done to quantify 'political risk' with respect to international or foreign investments and 'strike risk' has a similar political context. Neither international politics nor factory politics can seriously or realistically be forecast. Either the investor stays out of foreign investment and industrial investment or makes a considered judgment of certainties and uncertainties. If the judgment is to make the investment, he cannot then escape "exploitation" by the power of foreign government or trade union.

Contrary to Marxist and Leftist ideology, the more capitalistic either in amount of finance or technological interlocking assets, the more helpless is capital against such superior power from trade unionism or foreign etatism. Hutt has a conceptual logic at the macroeconomic level. As he notes, taxation can have limited effect in bringing about income transfers from the rich to poor but, he insists, the strike threat cannot. "Forcing up the price of labor in different firms, occupations or industries does not affect an income redistribution *from investors in general to workers in general.*" The italics are his but perhaps the meaning 'in general' does not in Hutt's presentation make sufficiently clear what the strike threat (and the strike) can do to income distribution in the particular. A non-Keynesian investor-entrepreneur might be permitted to murmur: in the long run I may be unexploited but I shall be bankrupt.

Throughout Hutt's formidable corpus of contribution to economic thought and policy prescription, there is the commitment to competition. It is an argument for economic pluralism to match political pluralism. The latter alone guarantees the individual voter democratic freedoms. Economic pluralism as a multiplicity of employers in market competition for workers, among other things, is a complex concept. Unlike collective bargaining, however, economic pluralism alone provides the individual workers with an effective guarantee against exploitation.

ON THE ECONOMICS
OF THE COLOUR BAR
by
Morgan O. Reynolds

To end whatever suspense might exist, let me assure the reader that I heartily approve of Professor Hutt's work on racial discrimination. But if these pages are to be even marginally productive, I must set my task at more than applause. Therefore, my purpose is to review and comment on *The Economics of the Colour Bar*,[1] assess its place in the wider literature on the economics of race, its place in Professor Hutt's work, and briefly discuss the unique constitutional problems of South Africa and Professor Hutt's proposal to deal with them.

Among the handful of truly great social issues, few rank higher than race relations. Although nationalism may be the strongest force in the world, race runs a close second. Both are forms of collective identity with enormous consequences. And there is a strong relationship between nationalism and race. South African exclusions of blacks, for instance, is like Western exclusion of guest workers and illegal immigrants, except that Europeans and Americans seem to exclude more.

Given these high stakes, the analysis of racial conflict deserves the most skilled and candid craftsmen. Of course, we have not been blessed with a consistently high order of scholars in this area. Most writers commit gross blunders, especially in economic matters, tend to rely on appeals to prejudice and emotion, and are more concerned about seizing the high moral ground than purusing the truth. For the most part, we have the situation described by H.L. Mencken: "What remains to the world, in the field of wisdom, is a series of long-tested and solidly agreeable lies." Fortunately, a few clear-eyed observers have turned their attention to race, not the least of which is W.H. Hutt.

Racial and ethnic differences ultimately involve the consensual bonds of a community. Neither freedom, peace, nor prosperity is possible without a relatively stable framework of laws, rules, and a degree of security for persons and property, a proposition demonstrated over and over again. Lebanon, Northern Ireland, Vietnam,— examples could be multiplied a hundredfold. A free, just, and stable regime depends on a minimal racial and ethnic accommodation. Professor Hutt shows the way for South Africa, the most complex and difficult case extant.

It is a privilege to write an essay in honor of Professor Hutt. I consider William Harold Hutt one of the great economists of our age. Although this opinion may not be widely shared within the economist's fraternity currently, the excellence of his work ultimately will be recognized. I am modest example of the converted. I only began to study Hutt's work when I started to study trade unions about nine years ago. The reason for this deficiency in my education is commonplace among economists of my vintage (43)—Hutt's work was never introduced in graduate programs.

Hutt's dogged and unswerving duty to the truth is his most outstanding virtue, as it should be for all scholars. But sound analysis is far more important. His excellence as an economist is highlighted by his failure to produce "negative knowledge." Much of the profession, in any era, is busy creating and propagating error. We have no better example of this than Hutt's great antagonist, John Maynard Keynes, whose clever yet superficial output was destructive in scientific terms and in its impact on public policy. Any discipline so susceptible to error, however, is insecure at its theoretical core. Perhaps Keynes' work was a form of creative destruction because it induced first-rate minds like Professor Hutt's to take up the challenge of the analytics of depression, unemployment, Say's principle, and similar matters. George Meany, past head of the AFL-CIO, has been quoted as saying that "The economics profession is the only one in which a man can rise to pre-eminence and never be right." Meany was right for once (with the possible exception of his own profession). In contemporary economics, admiration for mathematical muscle-flexing is so dominant that whether a theory or model has anything to do with something real is almost irrelevant. Professor Hutt suffers not at all from the ailment. He has been right on nearly everything; relevance and simplicity are his hallmarks.

Published in 1964, *The Economics of the Colour Bar* is Professor Hutt's major contribution to the analysis of race relations. Among his other papers on the same subject, the most important is "South Africa's Salvation in Classic Liberalism,"[2] published in 1972, an essay which succinctly states the political principles that Professor Hutt says are required to peacefully solve the seemingly intractable problem of race in the Republic of South Africa. It is an excellent companion to Hutt's *Colour Bar,* and I return to the constitutional question at the end of this essay.

The Economics of the Colour Bar consists of 189 pages divided into 18 short chapters. With only one table in the text, three tables in a statistical appendix, and no diagrams or equations, the book is accessible to virtually anyone. The subtitle, "A Study of the Economic Origins and Consequences of Racial Segregation in South Africa," admirably states the book's purpose. As Arnold Plant wrote in his 1965 review of the book in *Economic Journal:* "For anyone who wants to acquire, within the compass of a crime novel, a comprehensive understanding of the economic origins and consequences of racial segregation in South Africa (to quote Professor Hutt's sub-title), this is as good a book as he will find."[3]

Professor Hutt sets up the problem in his first chapter: to identify the forces that tend to dissolve the economic and social inferiority of non-whites, and the opposing forces which tend, deliberately or otherwise, to perpetuate racial inferiority. He describes the history of South Africa in compact and powerful terms. The first white settlement was established in Cape Town in 1652 by the Dutch East India Company as a half-way house to the East Indies. Dutch settlers, later known as Boers or Afrikaners, spread into the interior, though not by colonial design (as if by invisible hand?). The imported slaves, mainly from Malaya, and interbreeding between the two groups, later mixed with some African blood, produced the race known as Coloureds in South Africa today.

The British occupation dates from 1806, and the first settlers arrived in 1820. Despite the fact that the British brought a liberal and tolerant rule, with no attempt to suppress Afrikaner traditions or language, the Afrikaners were resentful and felt dominated. When the British abolished slavery in 1834, it triggered the "Great Trek" by bitter Afrikaner families into the interior. The Afrikaners defeated Black Africans along the trek and drove them into areas known as the reserves or "homelands." Further complicating the racial picture, the British imported large number of Indians between 1859 and 1911 for indentured labor on sugar plantations.

The political history of South Africa is no less messy than the racial picture. The Boer War broke out in 1899 and the victorious British brought the two independent Afrikaner republics (Orange Free State and the Transvaal) under British rule in 1902, and by 1910 the four independent colonies (Orange Free, Transvaal, Natal, and the Cape) were merged into the Union of South Africa under a unitary constitution. Although the British connection then became relatively unimportant, it was crucial on race, because the Crown was constitutionally responsible for the political rights of non-whites.

In the hope of appeasing Afrikaner sentiment, the British passed the Statute of Westminster in 1931, which quietly removed the authority of the British Crown to protect nonwhite political rights. The South African Parliament moved further in this direction with the Status Act of 1934 amid reassurances about respecting nonwhite rights. Professor Hutt tried to arouse public opinion in 1937 via the *Cape Times,* arguing that the public had been misled and that the Constitution had been "carelessly torn up." Rebuked for irresponsibility at the time, the Afrikaner Nationalists finally obtained the upper hand in 1948 and quickly verified Professor Hutt's analysis by abolishing nonwhite voting rights and imposing Apartheid on the entire community. Instead of the "liberalism" of the Cape spreading to the rest of South Africa, as many had expected, Afrikaner traditions emerged triumphant.

The five major ethnic groups of South Africa—Afrikaners, English-speaking Whites, Blacks, Coloured, and Indians—have staggering differences in their incomes, schooling, culture, and customs. Professor Hutt makes two powerful comments about the origins of racial bigotry among these groups. First, people from each group resent injustices toward themselves, yet the victims commonly favor the same injustices applied to other groups. Second, Hutt believes that economic status is crucial in determining prejudice, rather than vice versa. In other words, although there is a two-way dependence, the predominant relation is for prejudice to diminish as members of an inferior group make economic progress.[4] Professor Hutt also points out that discrimination is strongly conservative in that it stems from "hostility toward interlopers," that is, from the natural bent of incumbents to defend their economic privileges.

Although Professor Hutt puts its as gently as possible, it is clear from his account that Afrikaners and their racist ideology were the primary villains. Their history is filled with bitterness, comparative isolation from outside influence (partly due to language), and an uncompromising Calvinism. One aspect of this was the historical problem of the "Poor Whites," which might be described as the sin of pride. Afrikaners who were drawn into mining and urban employment from farming had little in the way of skills, yet they were too proud to start at the bottom of the Industrial ladder. Economic protectionism for them was an important ingredient in the political support for colour bars.

With the racial and political facts in place, the rest of the book is predominantly economic in character. In the late 1860s and early 1870s, diamond and gold discoveries led to huge amounts of Western investment in mining, which also stimulated railroad, engineering, and manufacturing development. The high demand for skilled labor attracted whites from abroad, while the demand for unskilled labor brought many Africans into the modern sector. Naturally, wage differentials were enormous. Whites were paid at world wage rates, while tribal blacks were paid what their minimal skills and relatively abundant supply warranted in the new world of the white man.

Throughout his analysis Professor Hutt emphasizes the constant probing of capitalists for the lowest cost means of production. Given huge wage differentials in the prices of skilled and unskilled labor services, sometimes exceeding 20 to 1, lower costs meant opening up employment opportunities for blacks. Yet this powerful incentive for investors and businessmen to invest in skills for Africans was constantly frustrated by interference from unions and by government restrictions.

Skilled white immigrants had brought the traditions of white trade unionism with them. This protectionist mentality, plus prejudice and a belief in "customary" differentials, was a potent political force on behalf of the status quo. Strike violence in the mines and railroads led to the first colour bar act, the Mines and Works Act of 1911, which was designed to appease an odd coalition of socialists, trade unions, and Afrikaners. The legislation delegated governmental action to administrative discretion, and the regulations actually adopted prohibited Africans from serving in a variety of mining occupations and in most other occupations specified ratios between foremen (Whites) and laborers (Africans). The legislation of 1911 was the first state-authorized coercion intended to deliberately restrain the tendency of markets to break down the nonmarket obstacles to equality of opportunity.

The Act of 1911 was only the first in a series of Labor Regulations which continue to hamper the South African economy to this day, though in attenuated form. Following the strike on the Rand in 1922, which developed into a virtual armed rebellion, the Industrial Conciliation Act was passed in 1924, the Wage Act in 1925, and the Mines and Works Act in 1926. Although these interventions restrained improvement in the standard of living of nonwhites, they were widely praised by collectivists as part of the 'civilized labor' era. Professor Hutt patiently describes the governmental appeasement which sheltered white unions and Afrikaners from nonwhite competition as only an economist who had taught at the University of Cape Town since 1928 could have.

Professor Hutt is careful to point out

that nonwhites have made a great deal of material progress since mining began, although they started from an extremely low point. A substantial share of their progress was due to entrepreneurial evasions of state restrictions. His main emphasis, though, is that nonwhite incomes could have risen much more rapidly, which would have had the important side-effect of enhancing their prestige and making it more difficult to exclude them from a share of political power.

The latter part of the book discusses the authoritarian system of controls—pass laws, influx controls, urban settlement, property ownership, and employment restrictions—which shackle economic progress and sustain Apartheid. Although South Africa has an Act for the Suppression of Communism, Professor Hutt points out that its labor controls are remarkably similar to those behind the Iron Curtain. Collectivism is collectivism, regardless of ideological hue. Chapters 16 and 17 discuss the ill-fated experiments in "separate development," or autarky, which persist today on the reserves. Again, a staggering array of discriminatory legal treatments toward both white and blacks attempts to isolate blacks and restrain the color-blind operation of the market. The final chapter sums up Professor Hutt's argument: the market liberates minorities and disadvantaged groups by offering new opportunities, while government interventions only benefits politically powerful interests, thereby retarding overall prosperity and preserving racial inequality.

An important mark of a good economist is careful definition, especially if normative or emotive terms like "injustice" are used. At the outset of his book Professor Hutt asks, "Why do the non-white peoples of the world today enjoy a much lower average standard of material well-being than the white peoples?" (p. 9). His answer is that "usually there is a mixture of causes... natural handicaps and...injustices at the hands of white people." Many of us raise our eyebrows when a term like injustice is invoked, but Professor Hutt assuages the skeptic's fears by precisely defining what he means by injustice on the same page: "Any policy which is intended to perpetuate the inferiority of material standards or status of any racial group."

Professor Hutt's willingness to embrace a normative word like injustice is revealing. His ultimate aim is not science for its own sake, but knowledge for the sake of clarifying public controversies and improving government's policies. He is unwilling to conceal his purpose, an admirable trait which surfaces in many ways. For instance, he is the only economist I know of who refers to "the authority of orthodox economics," though it is an accurate, even powerful phrase. It is a style from a bygone era. So much the worse for the world. Another sign of Professor Hutt's classical heritage occurred at the Mont Pelerin Society meetings when he was discussing union wage aggression with me and said, "It is their (manager's) moral duty to protect the consumers." This would strike many economists, heavily tooled in non-altruistic maximization techniques, as a peculiar, even naive comment. Yet I suspect that morale plays a strong but poorly understood role in economic affairs. Alfred North Whitehead said, "A great society is a society in which men of business think greatly of their functions." And if businessmen are ashamed of their functions, we suffer economic woes. Another example of Professor Hutt willingness to combine economics and ethics is his often repeated comment that "All man-made scarcities are wrong and reflect extortion." The emphasis on morality reminds me of R.H. Coase's recent tribute to Warren Nutter: "Warren Nutter was an excellent economist, which is rare, but he was something rarer still, a truly moral man."[5] I wish that I had written this about W.H. Hutt because it captures his qualities so well.

Hutt's stress on morality might be criticized as a threat to scientific understanding. The objection would be mistaken.

Professor Hutt has the highest possible regard for the truth and its pursuit. He only believes that economic analysis has a use beyond objective understanding. An interesting facet of his love of practical relevance is that it falsifies the objection from the Left and many undergraduate students who argue that orthodox, neoclassical economics is "afraid" to analyze the real problems. The truth in their attack on orthodox economics is that many economists find it more comfortable to stay clear of policy relevance. Hutt does not.

Hutt's analysis of the market's benign effect on racial inferiority is entirely correct. Lacking sins of commission to criticize, are there any sins of omission? A small infraction occurs, because Professor Hutt's book does not make a sufficiently strong case for the generality of his analysis. It is largely left up to readers to fill in their own applications beyond South Africa. Few have done it, I can safely assert, because contrary evidence has been scarce in the twenty years since publication. Although Professor Hutt explicitly points out that the lessons of the colour bar are general, it is only a gentle undercurrent in the book. It would have been valuable to draw the wider lessons and name names, dates, and places. Since Professor Hutt tried to address an audience beyond economists, especially the well-intended opponents of racial discrimination and Apartheid, generality would have measurably strengthened the book's influence.

An illustration of the wide applicabilty of the lessons in Professor Hutt's book is the debate over whether the industrial revolution was "worthwhile."[6] Although the question may seem absurd, few questions apparently fall in this category any longer, and it rages in the journals. The South African case is a contemporary re-enactment of the industrial revolution, and shows the immediate material advance which rural, nay primitive, peoples experience via mining employment, not to mention safer urban and manufacturing employments. The black immigration into South Africa, where a majority of mining employment is held by non-South Africans, puts a fine point on the matter through the best evidence of all, voting with their feet.

A good example of the incurable Left and their inability to grasp the lessons of the industrial revolution or to understand markets in South Africa is the 1965 book review by J.P. Nieuwenhuysen.[7] Professor Nieuwenhuysen was "far from convinced that the book succeeds in its author's principal (and ambitious) task." Accusing Hutt of "both a wrong diagnosis and prescription for the cure of economic injustice in South Africa and elsewhere," Nieuwenhuysen wrote that "interference with the operation of the 'free enterprise system' or 'market mechanism' is the only reason he (Hutt) adduces to explain the present marked inequalities of income and other injustices in South Africa." This sentence is evidence that the reviewer was too preoccupied to read what Professor Hutt had written. Professor Hutt always credits the inheritance of inferior circumstances, unattributable to any direct human intervention, as a factor in income differences. Professor Nieuwenhuysen, taken at his word apparently believes that inequalities of income, by themselves, are an injustice. Perhaps he also believes that all differences in outcomes of games of skill, of which market earnings are only an example, are "unjust." Nieuwenhuysen's biggest objection to the book is that "the problem seems much more complex than Professor Hutt makes it out to be, and its solution surely requires an answer less simple than 'the philosophy of free enterprise'." Why is it that people who propose the answer of centralized state power to solve social questions always accuse their opponents of being simple-minded? Professor Nieuwenhuysen's parting comment mocks a liberalism which depends on "the type of competitive economy now pretty well extinct."

The sole remark in the *Colour Bar* that I found confusing was Professor Hutt's observation about an alleged monopsony in the collective bargaining organization of the mining companies (p. 49). Professor Hutt claims that it is the "only unquestionable instance of labour-purchasing monopsony of which I know." But rather than "exploiting labour," it had the effect of ensuring a greater and more regular labour supply by overcoming the high "leisure preference" of Africans, according to Professor Hutt. This reference to the monopsony model is unfortunate, as far as I can tell, because the formal model of a monopoly buyer (or buyer's cartel) posits a buyer who faces the entire labor supply schedule and who in principle, pays a wage rate below the marginal cost of labor. I am unsure about what Professor Hutt really meant. Perhaps it has something to do with the form of compensation which allowed mining companies to "twist" the income leisure trade-off that Africans made. The reference to monopsony is simply too elliptical, although Professor Hutt refers to the technique as "educative." He also points out that farm squatting and the reserves were relevant alternatives to mining employment. An occasional problem in Professor Hutt's work is that the reasoning and evidence are too sparse to evaluate.

In assessing the place of *The Economics of the Colour Bar* in the literature on the economics of race, the publication date, 1964, is noteworthy. What existed by economists then? Not much. Nearly without exception, economists had ignored the issue until Gary Becker's, *The Economics of Discrimination* (1957).[8] Becker's book is still *the* book in the field, probably because it was first; indeed it was entirely novel at the time, and was outstanding in terms of technical sophistication. Lester Thurow wrote as late as 1969, "Current knowledge about the theory of discrimination rests almost entirely on the work of Gary Beck (1957)," a comment which perhaps says more about what economists know than about what is known.[9] As a graduate student at the University of Wisconsin in the late 60s, Becker's innovative work had deeply impressed me too.

Curiously, Professor Hutt does not mention the Becker book. Professor Hutt does quote a passage from Milton Friedman's discussion of discrimination in *Capitalism and Freedom*. Friedman refers to Becker's book, so Professor Hutt surely was aware of Becker's book. Why the oversight? I don't know, but it suggests something. Friedman had argued that free markets offer protection and opportunity to unpopular groups by offering powerful financial incentives to separate efficiency from irrelevant characteristics. Hutt does the same, but in greater detail, with more evidence, and in stronger terms. The Becker volume, on the other hand, is essentially mistaken, in my opinion. It postulates models of the international trade or "bloc" type to isolate the source of equilibrium segregation and racial wage differentials in markets. But the models are remarkably unsuccessful. They always imply unexploited profit opportunities via employment of the cheaper services of minority suppliers. Becker never satisfactorily addresses the question of why discriminatory equilibria would persist in markets. The empirical evidence for multitudes of profit-seekers is overwhelming, yet Becker fails to show why their activities don't undermine the effects of discriminators.[10] So, we could ask, why would Professor Hutt want to cite something that was basically in error in terms of market relevance, even though Becker's work contributes to our theoretical understanding?

Professor Hutt wrote his journalistic diagnosis of colour bars, especially that most subtle colour bar of all which holds back the advance of Africans-"the rate for the job"-long before the now-celebrated Becker book. Hutt's book however, did not appear until 1964, robbing it of some of the thunder it might otherwise have had. Since then, of course, we have been flooded with literature on the economics of discrimination, sex, and race, some of it excellent and rigorous work. The work of Sowell, Williams, Fogel and Engerman, among many others, deserves mention. Their work was eased because they could build on the work of giants like Professor Hutt, though I am afraid Hutt has been slighted by most authors. This may be due to, among other things, the fact that Americans generally are unacquainted and uninterested in Africa. But it is worth mentioning that most American economists fail to cite *The Economics of the Colour Bar,* including Ray Marshall's 1974 survey.[11]

In my judgment the book most closely related to Professor Hutt's book is *Competition and Coercion* by Robert Higgs.[12] This is an excellent book about American Blacks in the South form 1865 to 1914. Professor Higgs, like Hutt, believes that economic issues cannot be treated outside of their social, legal, and political context, lest we be led seriously astray. In remarkably similar words to Professor Hutt, Higgs says, "Black economic history in the half century after emancipation makes sense only when interpreted as an interplay of two systems of behavior: a competitive economic system and a coercive racial system" (p. 13).

With dexterity, Higgs clarifies the problem with Professor Becker's models and touches on the reason that Professor Hutt could ignore Becker's work:

In fact, during the period 1865-1914, the legislation of the Southern states proba-

bly mattered less than the refusal of the whites who controlled the legal machinery to provide equal protection to the blacks. This allowed a reign of 'private' lawlessness, intimidation, and violence that had pervasive effects on the economic behavior of the blacks. By virtue of the public sector's complicity in these actions, 'private' coercion and persecution were indirectly aspects of what Becker calls 'collective discrimination'; but he has not chosen to incorporate such elements into his analysis. To do so would complicate the model considerably, but perhaps an inelegant analysis of a central problem would be more valuable than a rigorous analysis of a peripheral issue. (p. 10).

The unfortunate truth, however, is that if we measure "more valuable" by faculty salaries, rigorous (read: mathematical) analysis of peripheral issues pays considerably more than inelegant analysis of central problems.[13]

I would be remiss if the 1982 book by Kantor and Rees, *South African Economic Issues*, were not mentioned also.[14] This book covers a gamut of economic issues, including macroeconomic issues, monetary policy, and international trade, while Hutt's book is strictly microeconomic. The Kantor/Rees analysis of South African labor markets, however, is sound and up-

dates Professor Hutt's book. They point
out that influx controls were strenuously
enforced in South Africa but should be regarded like the immigration controls of
other countries, and that much of second-
ary industry was not permitted to hire mi-
grant labor. Following the Wiehahn
Commission report (1979) there has been a
definite loosening of restrictions on black
employment, residence, and training.
Kantor/Rees argue that colour bars in the
mines applied only to specific industries
and cannot serve as a general explanation
of racial income differences. The ratio of
Blacks to Whites has increased in all important sectors of the economy, including
mining, while wage differentials have sig-
nificantly narrowed in the last ten years.[15]
Job reservation never amounted to more
than a small number of jobs, though the
possibility of further job reservation in-
hibits substitutions of Black for White labor. Governmental intervention on behalf
of dissatisfied white workers adds an element of uncertainty in South Africa. But
substantial change is underway in South
African labor markets, sometimes in surprising directions.[16]

Professor Hutt's main point is that all
collectivist systems and state planning are
alike. Political majorities, often badly dis-
torted by voting mechanisms and logroll-
ing, exploit political minorities, even

though the political minorities may represent population majorities. Nowhere is the general problem of constitutional change more pressing than in South Africa, nor is there any better essay to read as a blueprint toward reform than Professor Hutt's "South Africa's Salvation in Classic Liberalism" (see footnote 2).

Political power is a constant zero sum game. Hence, the expression "sharing political power" is well chosen. White fears are two-fold: Sharing of power with Nonwhites risks loss of existing White privileges, and secondly, risks a drastic redistribution of wealth in a "winner-take-all" cataclysm. Even journalists have learned something from the last twenty years of experience in black Africa, where African socialism has spread penury and no black leader has been peacefully voted out of office.[17]

Professor Hutt says that South Africa has to be better than the rest of the world. This observation is true but discouraging. Professor Hutt, however, insists that his political platform is not impossible. It would take time, and gradualism is the essence of his wise counsel. He advises the state to return to its primary function, namely, to ensure the freedom of men in thought, communication, and action by suppressing all private use of coercive power. In an era where people are accustomed to governments as multibillion-dollar subsidy clearing houses, restoration of such rectitude is especially difficult. And in South Africa, where the burden of accumulated grievance and fear is especially great, the problem is even worse.

Professor Hutt is like Milton Friedman in his approach to policy questions. Both men are indefatigably optimistic and offer their prescriptions without a trace of despair. Professor Hutt writes, "Under a Constitution which is at least conceivable, with strong entrenched and strict enforcement, the supposed 'miracle' of good relations under freedom in a racially complex society is not beyond attainment."[18] By contrast, Professor Stigler insists that until we understand the political process, we are poorly equipped to influence it. The merit of Professor Hutt's contribution, however, is that he offers a reasoned demonstration of how to solve the problem, whether or not the political process can actually converge on it. Professor Hutt's assessment about the likelihood of his recommended outcome is that it is "Very remote were it not for the obvious fact that the existing political and economic situation cannot indefinitely endure."[19]

W.H. Hutt is a classical political economist who has brilliantly applied and refined economic theory in a variety of contexts. His work on the economics of race is an outstanding contribution to that literature, though it is not his most outstanding contribution to economics. Fortunately, we can have all his work and need not sacrifice any of it. In Professor Hutt's lifetime work, his *Economics of the Colour Bar* displays his fearless courage, demonstrates the power of simple economic theory in the hands of a master, reinforces the unity of his work, and once again verifies that the release of market restraints is the means to maximum employment and output. Capitalism is the solution, not the problem.

1. W. H. Hutt, *The Economics of the Colour Bar* (London: Andre Deutsch for The Institute of Economics Affairs, 1964).

2. ____, "South Africa's Salvation in Classic Liberalism," pp. 103-25, *Studies in Economics and Economic History,* edited by Marcelle Kooy (Durham, NC.: Duke University Press, 1972).

3. Arnold Plant, "Review of *The Economics of the Colour Bar,*" *Economic Journal,* 75 (December 1965), p. 827.

4. Arthur Shenfield beautifully illustrates how capitalism nurtures and reinforces just and good behavior in

"Capitalism Under The Test of Ethics," pp. 55-65 in *Homage to Mises,* edited by John K. Andrews, Jr. (Hillsdale, MI: Hillsdale College Press, 1981).

5. R.H. Coase, *How Should Economists Choose?* (Washington: American Enterprise Institute for Public Policy Research, 1982), p. 5.

6. Jeffrey G. Williamson, "Was The Industrial Revolution Worth It?," *Explorations in Economic History,* 19 (July 1982), pp. 221-45.

7. J.P. Nieuwenhuysen, "Review of *The Economics of the Colour Bar,"* South African Journal of Economics,* 33 (June 1965), pp. 164-65.

8. Gary S. Becker, *The Economics of Discrimination* (Chicago: The University of Chicago Press, 1957).

9. Lester Thurow, *Poverty and Discrimination* (Washington: The Brookings Institution, 1969), p. 112.

10. Joseph Stiglitz highlights the special conditions which international trade models (Black and Whites as separate countries) require to prevent resource price equalization in "Approaches to the Economics of Discrimination," *American Economic Review,* 63 (May 1973), pp. 287-95. Marxists models especially depend on the assumption that labor markets are segmented; see

Glen G. Cain, "The Challenge of Segmented Labor Market Theories To Orthodox Theory: A Survey," *Journal of Economic Literature,* 14 (December 1976), pp. 1215-57.

11. Ray Marshall, "The Economics of Racial Discrimination: A Survey," *Journal of Economics Literature,* 12 (September 1974), pp. 849-71.

12. Robert Higgs, *Competition and Coercion* (London: Cambridge University Press for the Hoover Institution, 1977).

13. Wassily Leontief, a Nobel prizewiner in economics, wrote in a letter to *Science* (July 9, 1982): "Page after page of professional economic journals are filled with mathematical formulas leading the reader from sets or more or less plausible but entirely abritrary assumptions to precisely stated but irrelevant conclusions." To support his point, Leontief surveyed the articles in the *American Economic Review* for the last ten years and found that a majority were mathematical models without any data.

14. Brian Kantor and David Rees, *South African Economic Issues* (Cape Town: Juta & Co. Ltd., 1982).

15. See, for instance, the narrowing Black/White earnings differentials reported in *South Africa 1982,* Offical

Yearbook of the Republic of South Africa (Johanneseberg: Chris Van Rensburg, 1982), pp. 474-75. The black share of total labor income grew from 20.1 to 29.8 percent between 1970 and 1979, while the White share fell from 70.1 to 59.0 percent (p. 335).

16.   See, for instance, the ironic turnabout occurring among the unions in "White South Africa Miners See Grouping with Black Unions as Safeguard on Jobs," *The Wall Street Journal,* (November 5, 1982), p. 27.

17.   Xan Smiley, "Misunderstanding Africa," *The Atlantic Monthly,* (September 1982), pp. 70-79.

18.   "South Africa's Salvation . . . ," p. 122.

19.   Ibid.

MAJOR CONTRIBUTIONS BY PROFESSOR W.H. HUTT

(1) BOOKS

The Theory of Collective Bargaining (London: Staples, 1930), 2nd Edition, 1977, I.E.A., 2nd Edition, 1977, Cato Institute.

Economists and the Public (London: Jonathan Cape, 1936).

The Theory of Idle Resources (London: Jonathan Cape, 1939).

Plan for Reconstruction (London: Kegan Paul, 1943).

Keynesianism—Retrospect and Prospect (Chicago: Regnery, 1963).

The Economics of the Colour Bar (London: Deutsch, 1964).

Neo-Keynesianism and Academic Freedom (Tokyo: Yoyo Keizai, 1966).

Politcially Impossible...? (London: Institute of Economic Affairs, 1971).

The Strike-Threat System (Arlington, Va.: Arlington House, 1973).

A Rehabilitation of Say's Law (Athens: Ohio University Press, 1975).

The Keynesian Episode: A Reassessment (Indianapolis: Liberty Press, 1979).

(2) ARTICLES

"The Factory System of the Early Nineteenth Century," *Economica* (March 1926), pp. 78-93.

"Economic Aspects of the Report of the Poor White Commission," *South African Journal of Economics (S.A.J.E.)* (September 1933), pp. 281-90.

"The Significance of State Interference With Interest Rates," *S.A.J.E.* (September 1933), pp. 365-68.

"Economic Method and the Concept of Competition," *S.A.J.E.* (March 1934), pp. 1-23.

"Co-ordination and the Size of the Firm," *S.A.J.E.* (December 1934), pp. 383-402.

"Logical Issues in the Study of Industrial Legislation," *S.A.J.E.* (March 1935), pp. 26-42.

"Natural and Contrived Scarcities, *S.A.J.E.* (September 1935), pp. 345-53.

"The Nature of Aggressive Selling," *Economica* (August 1935), pp. 298-320.

Review of J. Hilton and others: *Are Trade Unions Obstructive? Economica* (November 1935).

"Discrimination Monopoly and the Consumer," *Economic Journal,* (March 1936), pp. 61-79.

"The Price Mechanism and Economic Immobility," *S.A.J.E.* (September 1936), pp.

319-30.

"Economic Aspects of the Report of the Cape Coloured Commission," *S.A.J.E.* (June 1938), pp. 117-33.

"Pressure Groups and *Laissez-Faire*," *S.A.J.E.* (March 1938), pp. 1-23.

"Privacy and Private Enterprise," *S.A.J.E.* (December 1939), pp. 375-88.

"Economic Lessons of the Allied War Effort," *S.A.J.E.* (September 1940), pp. 205-13.

"The Concept of Consumers' Sovereignty," *Economic Journal* (March 1940), pp. 66-77.

"Economic Institutions and the New Socialism," *Economica* (November 1940), pp. 419-34.

"Distributive Justice," *S.A.J.E.* (September 1941), pp. 219-34.

"War Demand, Entrepreneurship and the Distributive Problem," *Economica* (November 1941), pp. 341-60.

"The Price Factor and Reconstruction" (with R. Leslie), *S.A.J.E.* (December 1941), pp. 441-44.

"The Sanctions for Privacy Under Private Enterprise," *Economica* (August 1942), pp. 237-44.

"A Critique of the First Report of the Social and Economic Planning Council," *S.A.J.E.* (March 1943), pp. 48-62.

"The Concept of Waste," *S.A.J.E.* (March 1943), pp. 1-10.

"Public Works and Reconstruction," *S.A.J.E.* (September 1943), pp. 198-209.

"Two Studies in the Statistics of Russia," *S.A.J.E.* (March 1944), pp. 18-42.

"Plan for Economic Research in the Union," *S.A.J.E.* (June 1944), pp. 81-100.

"Full Employment and the Future of Industry," *S.A.J.E.* (September 1945), pp. 185-202.

"Further Aspects of Russian Statistics," *S.A.J.E.* (December 1945), pp. 344-63.

"The Development of the Soviet Economic System," *S.A.J.E.* (September 1946), pp. 215-19.

The Sterling Area: Financial Position of the Union of South Africa, University of London and Institute of Bankers, 1949.

"The Nature of Money," *S.A.J.E.* (March 1952), pp. 50-64.

"The Notion of the Volume of Money," *S.A.J.E.* (1952), pp. 231-41.

"The Notion of Money of Constant Value," *S.A.J.E.* (September 1953), pp. 215-26, and (December 1953), pp. 341-53.

"The Significance of Price Flexibility," *S.A.J.E.* (March 1954), pp. 727-30.

"The Yield on Money Held," in *Freedom and Free Enterprise,* ed. Sennholz, 1954.

"New Light on Wicksell," *S.A.J.E.* (March 1959), pp. 38-42.

"A Question of Stereotypes," *Fortune Magazine,* 1963.

"The Critics of Classical Economics,"

S.A.J.E. (June 1964), pp. 81-94.

"Keynesian Revisions," *S.A.J.E.* (June 1965), pp. 101-13.

"South Africa's Salvation in Classic Liberalism," *Il Politico,* 1965, No. 4, pp. 782-95.

"Keynes: Obsolete But Influential," *The Wall Street Journal* (September 1965).

"Unanimity Versus Non-Discrimination (as Criteria for Constitutional Validity)," *S.A.J.E.* (June 1966), pp. 133-47.

"Civil Rights and Young 'Conservatives'," *Modern Age* (Summer 1966), pp. 231-38.

"Twelve Thoughts on Inflation," *New Individualist Review* (Winter 1967).

"Economic Position of the Bantu in South Africa," in *Western Civilization and the Natives of South Africa,* ed. I. Schapera (New York: Humanities Press, 1967).

"Misgivings and Causistry on Strikes," *Modern Age* (Fall 1968), pp. 350-60.

"The Rhodesian Calumny," *New Individualist Review* (1968).

"Economics of Immigration," in *Symposium on Immigration,* ed. A. Plant (London: Institute of Economic Affairs, 1972), pp. 19-44.

"The Poor Who Were With Us," *Encounter* (November 1972), pp. 84-90.

"South Africa's Solution in Classical Liberalism," in *Symposium: Essays on Economics and Economic History,* ed. M. Kooy (London: MacMillan, 1972).

"Illustration of Keynesianism," *Politically Impossible?*, 1971.

"Where Do We Go From Keynes?," *National Review*, 1975.

"Economic Power and Labor Unions". Paper delivered at the Association for Social Economy meeting, New York, 1973. (ed. Pejovich and Klingman), *Individual Freedom*, 1975.

"The Market Mechanism in a Free Enterprise System" *Free Markets, Law, and Free People:* Proceedings of a Conference jointly presented by the University of Texas at Arlington, Center for Business Research, Arlington, Texas, 1977.

"Every Man A Capitalist," *Policy Review*, 1982.

"Razing Keynes: An Economist for the Long Run," *Wall Street Journal*, 1983.

"The Face and Mask of Unionism," *Journal of Labor Research*, 1983.

A NOTE ON CONTRIBUTORS

THOMAS HAZLETT, an assistant professor of agricultural economics at the University of California, Davis, received his Ph.D. in economics from UCLA in 1984. He is the author of articles in economics journals, senior editor of *Manhattan Report,* and contributing editor to *Reason Magazine.*

RALPH HORWITZ a former student of W.H. Hutt, received his degree in Commerce from University of Cape Town. He served as chief executive of a publishing company and editor-in-chief of the group periodicals. He has written extensively on public affairs and management subjects and served as Lecturer in Economics and Visiting Professor at universities in Britain and the United States. Dr. Horwitz currently resides in Great Britain.

CONNIE M. MORAN is currently an Instructor of Economics at Georgetown University in Washington, D.C., where she attended the School of Foreign Service and is completing her doctoral studies in International Economics. A recipient of a Fulbright Graduate Fellowship for 2 years, Ms. Moran conducted research on European Economic Integration at the Institute of World Economics at the University of Kiel in West Germany. While she is presently affiliated with the U.S. Department of State, she has also held short-term positions at the International Monetary Fund and the American Enterprise Institute for Public Policy Research.

MORGAN O. REYNOLDS, a professor of economics at Texas A&M University, received his Ph.D. from the University of Wisconsin in 1971. He is the author of many articles in academic journals and of three books: *Public Expenditures, Taxes, and the U.S. Distribution of Income* (1977), *Power and Privilege: Labor Unions in America* (1984), and *Crime by Choice* (1985). A forthcoming work is *Productivity and the Unions.*

ARTHUR A. SHENFIELD is an English economist and barrister. He is a former Economic Director of the Confederation of British Industry, and Director of the (British) Industrial Policy Group. He had previously been Assistant Editor of the London and Cambridge Economic Service and Lecturer in Economics at the University of Birmingham. A Lord Justice Holker Exhibitioner of Gray's Inn, he practised at the English Bar for ten years. In recent years he has been a Visiting Professor at various American Universities and Colleges. In 1972-74 he was President of the Mont Pelerin Society. From 1959 to 1984 he was External Examiner in the Economics of Industry at the University of London.